Lonely Girl

by

Robert W Fisk

A catalogue record for this book is available from the National Library of New Zealand.

Published by Foxburr Publishing
Mosgiel, New Zealand

DEDICATION

For Thomas and Magalie who taught me new tricks.

DISCLAIMER

This is a work of fiction. It has been created entirely by the author. Any resemblance to any person is coincidental as are the procedures and personnel in the organisations described.

COPYRIGHT© 2025

1.

She is three years and one week old, just a baby really. For her birthday, her grandparents give her a three-wheel tricycle but she is not allowed to ride it on the street without Mum or Grandad. Instead, she rides the trike around and around the small lawn at the front of the house by the road.

At the front fence, a man calls to her. He is a nice man, like Grandad.

"Hello," he calls. "What a lovely trike. What is its name?"

"Thally."

Last week there were balloons on the gate and several young boys and girls were playing in the garden.

"Is Sally a present?" he asks with a smile as he leans on the gate.

"Yeth. I am free."

The man thinks for a moment. "Three? What a grown-up girl. Why don't you ride on the pavement?"

"No. Only with Mum or Grandad."

"I'm a grandad. Can I take you for a ride?"

The little girl thinks seriously.

"Yeth."

"What's your name, dear?"

"Thally."

He opens the gate and Sally rides off with him.

2.

I am Lesley Smith. I am sitting on the stairs feeling happy because our new house is awesome.

Our new house is quite old. It has two bedrooms upstairs. Mine has an en suite bathroom. Dad uses the other bathroom next to his bedroom. There is also a lavatory downstairs. Dad cleans the three lavatories and his room. I do the rest of the house, which is a kitchen-diner and a reception room downstairs and my bedroom upstairs to the left. Dad's bedroom is on the right.

The house is made of brick. The windows have wooden frames and lift up and down, the old-fashioned kind people call sash windows. There is a staircase to get upstairs. For an older house, it is surprisingly bright inside. There is a cracked window that whistles in the wind. The landlord said he would fix it but so far, he hasn't. I hope he comes before school starts.

The house used to have a garden at the back but there is a new house there now and we have just a little piece of garden bed with shrubs and stuff. Dad says that means less work for us. As well as the house behind ours we have a house on each side. The road goes up, so the house on the right as you look at it is lower than ours and we are lower than the house on the left.

The houses are the same as ours with different coloured window frames and front door. Dad said they are both rented, like ours. There is an old man in the house above us, and two men in the house below. Dad and the men next door have cars that have to be parked on the street. The old man catches the bus that stops further up the hill on the other road.

I really hope we can stay here for a long time. Maybe our solid house will become a home for us. When I started a new school, I had to make new friends. I got bullied as well but that didn't last because I am tall.

I get teased because people think Lesley is a boy's name. Dad says Mum chose my name before she was killed in a car accident when I was three. I can't remember what she looked like but I can remember how she held me and cuddled me. I also remember her voice, especially when she tucked me up in bed after reading a story and said goodnight to Rupert my cuddly soft toy rabbit. I still have Rupert and he smells of Mum.

I am skinny but tall for my age. Most of the boys in my last class were shorter than me. Unlike Dad, I have fair skin and red hair. He says I take after Mum but he has no photos to show me. He says there was a fire and everything was destroyed.

Dad is tall and dark, with lovely hazel eyes. He loves me and has never hit me, not even when I have been really naughty. He has never brought a lady home, but when I do the washing, I sometimes smell perfume that tells me he has been with a woman.

I am eleven. I will be twelve in a week. When school starts, I will be in Year 8. I am not looking forward to my new school.

Dad took me there on Teachers Day, the Friday before the term begins. The school is on the other side of a lovely park. We walked to the school. Autumn was just beginning. Some leaves on the trees were turning colour but mainly they were still green. I got hot because I wore my new puffer jacket.

From the park you have to cross a busy road. There is a traffic light and a crossing and just along a little bit, the back pathway to the school, which is a mixture of old and new buildings. There was nobody around. We walked past the sprawling senior block. It was made of concrete, neat and tidy, no litter or junk. A man was using a long brush and a hose to clean the three levels of windows. He was getting wet.

Further on we came to a sign saying, Junior Block. That's me. Years Seven and Eight are in a lovely old building made of creamy stone. The metal framed windows are all in squares of nine, which makes ten if you count the whole window as a square. The Office is at the front of the building. We came from the back and had to walk past the building then turn left.

"Can we help you?" asked an older woman, maybe forty-ish, like Dad.

"I want to enrol my daughter, Lesley Smith," he said.

The secretary opened a large book. I can read upside down. The book had columns on her left for Name, Family name, Date of Birth and Address and phone. Dad enrolled me, showed the secretary my birth certificate, and said that as he is a crane driver working on the wharves and Mrs Smith has passed away, could I go to my new class on my own on Monday?

How embarrassing. I will be twelve in a week. I don't need a parent holding my hand and leading me to the classroom.

"Of course you can," she said. "Just wait, I'll get her class teacher, Miss Beech, to show her where to go."

Her? Not Lesley? From bad to worse.

Miss Beech came from the staff room with a cup of coffee in her hand. She seemed nice. She is three inches shorter than me. She looked a little chubby because of the tweedy sort of clothes she wore. Her hair was cut short to just below the collar of the button-up blouse she was wearing. She looked like someone's auntie. I wish I had an auntie. My fear lessened a little. But only a little.

After a little chat, we went to the classroom. Dad stood too close to Miss Beech but she didn't seem to mind.

I felt ignored.

Monday will be a horror day and I don't know anybody here.

3.

On Saturday I go for a walk. Dad comes with me. We walk to the nearby park that leads to the school but there is no one my age there. Dad thinks there might be some Year Eights at McDonald's but there aren't. It was a nice idea, Dad.

On Sunday the man in the house next door says hello to me. He is an old man, much older than Dad. He is a little bit stooped and moves slowly. He has a lovely garden, not like ours. I wouldn't go into the garden to see the flowers at the back of the house. I stood on the pavement while he went and cut me some lovely flowers for the house.

I didn't think I would be able to sleep but while I was counting backwards from a hundred, I dozed off.

On Monday morning I feel tired. My eyes are itchy and they have crusts in each corner. I listen. I hear the lock on Dad's bedroom open with a light rattle. I know my door will be next. Dad will pop his head in and say, "How's my Poppet? Ready for X?" X might be swimming, shopping, or a visit somewhere. Today it is school and I don't need any reminding.

Poppet. Yuk. I roll my eyes in despair.

My door opens. Dad's head appears above the bed covers. "How's my Poppet? Ready for school?

"You look tired, Poppet," he says but his voice shows no sympathy and his eyes say, "You are going whether you like it or not."

"Pancakes with syrup?"

I love pancakes with maple syrup. We sit at the kitchen bar and eat together.

"You alright going on your own?" Dad asks as he gives me my cut lunch of sandwiches and fruit.

"Sure. I'll manage."

"Walk or come in the car with me?"

Going with Dad would get me to school an hour early. It would also look like Dad had to take me to school. I wouldn't meet anyone. I want to make friends which means walking so people can talk to me.

"No. I'll walk. Thanks Dad," I say as he kisses my forehead. He is a good Dad.

I'll spend the hour vacuuming the living room. Then I'll talk to Mum through Rupert Rabbit. I'll ask her what to do to make friends. I seem to make friends quickly but they don't stay friends for long. Rupert Rabbit is my secret; if anyone knows I can talk to Mum through a toy rabbit they'll lock me up as a crazy.

Suddenly I remember that the school is ten minutes away – by CAR! I think it will take me twenty minutes to get there if I run through the park

I hurry down the street, turn right go along to the gates, and then walk through the park. I run for a short distance. With a backpack and wearing a school blazer, I start to sweat. I don't want to be smelly or sweaty so I go back to walking.

A girl dressed in a blazer overtakes me on her bicycle. She stops. Her name is Rose Knowles. She is short and small. She is in my class and says she will walk with me. We arrive ten minutes late. I am grateful to Rose for being with me when I am late.

Our footsteps seem to ring in the corridor. There is nobody around but us. Everyone is in class. We come to the classroom door. It has a glass panel in it, I suppose so the Principal can look and see if all is well. Miss Beech sees me and waves me in.

"Hello Rose. Thank you for helping Lesley find us. Class, this is Lesley Smith, a new pupil. Be friendly to her please."

Miss Beech is friendly. I am pleased Dad and I visited the school on Friday. There are two seats free in the second block of seats. Rose and I sit down and pay attention.

Miss Beech is making some rules. She explains how she wants our exercise books set out. I feel a ping on my ear. It is a small wad of paper, fired from a rubber band. I turn and glare at the people behind me. A large boy with a round face is staring innocently at the ceiling. I think it was him but the people near him are smirking and giggling. I decide to make a fuss.

"Ow!"

I rub my ear with one hand and stare at the wad of paper I hold in my other hand.

I thought Miss Beech would be a pushover but she is quick and firm.

"Lesley, don't make such a fuss. Hayden Millard. Go to the Office."

"I'll get you," he threatens as he moves past me.

I don't think I am making any friends. Because I made a fuss and Hayden Millard got sent to the Office nobody will talk to me. When we work in pairs or groups everyone avoids me. Except Rose.

We go through maths, reading and writing then we have our school lunch. I don't qualify for a free lunch because dad is earning a good wage. He hasn't paid for me yet so I take my own lunch today.

I take my sandwiches from my backpack and follow the others to the canteen. I see Hayden Millard coming towards us as he pushes through against the current. What does he want?

I am frightened but stand up to him. He grabs my lunch, drops it to the floor and stamps on it. Everyone stops still and silent, watching, calculating. This is a challenge. If I back down I am dog food. I need a friend.

"Hey, Millard. Stop that."

I turn and see a boy I know as Bill.

"Who's going to make me?" Millard answers.

People are looking, staring, or half turning away because Millard has challenged Bill.

"Me!" I roar, and race at Millard, hitting him with straight arms to his chest. Over he goes.

Everyone roars with laughter. Bill and I walk on as if nothing has happened. We sit together at a table for four. Just the two of us. Two girls join us.

"Hey girl, that was awesome. I'm Nancy. Nancy Drew, believe it or not. I'm a girl of colour so no-one sits with me. Hayden bullies us. Thanks for putting him down."

"Call me Rose the Nose," says the smaller girl. "'Cos, I stick my nose in where it doesn't belong."

Bill gives me the squashed sandwiches he has been carrying in his hand. I take the sandwiches. They are mush. The apple and the pear are fine. I cut them in half and tell my new friends to help themselves.

We are in different classes. Rose and I are in the same class with Miss Beech. Nancy Drew and Bill are in Miss Dean's class. We talk about Tuesday and Thursday Elective. We want to be together if we can. Bill seems very keen to be in the same elective as me.

There is quite a list, ranging from elementary martial arts, board games, and Harriers. We agree to meet at lunch tomorrow and join Civics.

What a funky group we are. Rose the Nose lives in a world of her own. Nancy feels rejected. I am lonely. I was home-schooled by an old lady until Year 7 but she died so I have only had one term in an ordinary school, Chaytor School, which I hated..

After school I see Bill. He tells me people call him Retard Taylor. I don't see why. He has brown skin and speaks slowly but he is not stupid. I like Bill. I will try to see more of him.

4.

As l walk home, I think of my new friends. I have never made friends so quickly. I am happy. I hope Dad doesn't have to find another job and we have to move house again.

As I walk through the park a bicycle overtakes me and then stops. Two bicycles stop behind me. In front of me is Hayden Millard. Behind me are two boys I don't know. Surrounded, I am frightened. I am big but I am a girl and even a strong boy like Bill couldn't handle three boys.

"What do you want Hayden?"

"We just want to see you safely home." says Hayden.

I do not want him to find out where I live so I reply, "Hayden, can it wait? Can you find someone else to bother? I have to go to the shops and I have to visit someone. I don't need any help."

"Oh yes you do. For a pound we will walk home with you, keeping you safe and out of danger of being robbed."

Stay calm. Appear to consider his offer. Use your height to make you look tougher than you are. "I am not giving you any money. I don't need your help."

"Then you have to pay us for being rude and not taking our offer."

The next moment one of the boys behind me grabs my backpack and slips it off my shoulders. It holds my exercise books and nothing else.

"Lost your bag, have you?" says the third boy. I later find his name is Ronald. He takes the backpack from the smaller boy. He hurls it across the pathway into some shrubs.

"I want two pounds for finding it. Oh, there it is."

They are tormenting me. They have my backpack. If I pay them, they will never stop demanding money. I am trapped and cannot escape.

"Hayden, please tell your friends to return my backpack, and please let me get on my way. I am never going to pay you so you might as well leave me alone."

I go behind the two bikes and cross to where the boy has thrown my bag. They weren't expecting me to go that way. I pick up my backpack, slip it on my back then start walking towards home. The three boys follow me. They call me names like Stuck Up. and the B word and worse. I am almost crying.

The small boy, Alan I think his name is, says, "Come on Hayden. Let's get out of here."

I see two ladies coming towards us. One is pushing a pram. The bullies see them.

"Yeah, Alan. Let's go."

They climb on their bikes and ride back the way they came.

"Are you alright, luv?" asks the woman pushing the pram.

I want to say, "No, I've just been frightened and threatened by three horrible inhuman boys." Instead, I say, "I have just had three boys try to bully me."

"Was that Hayden Millard one of them?" asks the older lady. She looks like the young woman; might be her mother.

My voice shakes a little. "Yes. I don't think I'll go home through the park in future."

"Don't you give in to them," says the young mother. "Get some friends to go home with you. Bullies are cowards at heart."

I am still shaking when Dad comes home at six o'clock. He is tired. While he is having his shower I serve dinner; chicken drumsticks with roast potatoes, peas and cabbage.

"You're an angel, Lesley, just like your mother," he says. I glow all over. He is a good Dad who always says wonderful things when I cook.

"Do you miss her, Dad?"

"Yes, all the time.'

"Are you going to marry again?"

"Only if I find someone like your mother. Meantime, I've got the next best thing. I've got you."

I feel good about that, all gooey and warm. I feel good all evening. We watch a little television. I do my homework while Dad reads a book.

"Dad, how do you deal with a bully?"

"You have to remain calm and reasonable. Find out why they bully. That will give you an idea of their weakness. You don't hit them. Just keep asking questions."

I think about that. I like Bill and I hate Hayden. Bill wants to be my partner in the Civics Elective. but I will choose Hayden Millard and find out what is wrong with him.

I clear the table, wash the dishes in the sink and stack them on the counter. Dad dries them and puts things away.

I go to my room and read in bed with Rupert Rabbit. I tell him about my new friends. I make him wiggle his ears to show he approves.

Half an hour later Dad locks my door and then I hear him lock his door as he goes to bed. He is scared of secret police raiding our house. I am scared he is paranoid.

I will ask Bill to walk home with me. I turn off my light and sleep.

<h1 style="text-align:center">5.</h1>

On Tuesday, we have Miss Beech all morning. She keeps interest high by explaining everything clearly. The class is settling into its daily routines. I have a problem with the homework she sets. She wants photos of us as babies. I don't have any. They were destroyed when the house burned down.

Dad paid my lunch bill by internet. The dining room is large and is filled with students. We eat first because we are younger and get out of class fifteen minutes earlier than Year Nines and older. I am told the dining room used to be a church hall. It now smells like a restaurant.

Restaurants and dining rooms sound and look alike, the smell of the food, the hushed waves of conversation, and the rows of tables. I see an empty table for four. I hope I can get it before anyone else sits there.

I join the line, pick up a plate; mashed potatoes, vegetarian meat substitute – I must buy some this afternoon – carrots, something that looks like cabbage and nauseous gravy. I try to stop the gravy but the lady behind the bench is on auto mode and slaps gravy over my food anyway. Bread. I pick up two slices. I must buy bread today.

Someone sits at the table I want. I move through the spaces between tables and find the person sitting is Rose Knowles. Rose the Nose. She has no food in front of her. Bill comes next. Most boys are shy with girls because other boys will tease them. Bill seems not to mind. Sailing through the crowd of people near the counter, Nancy Drew is a cruise liner cutting through the waves. I don't know how she got served so quickly.

"Easy," she laughs. "Mum is a friend of a server so she gets a plate ready for me with everything on it. I leave what I don't want.

Rose still hasn't gone for her food.

"What's wrong, Rose?" I ask.

"Mum can't pay for lunches until payday," she says. I haven't touched my food with its glue for gravy. I slip it in front of her.

"Have mine," I tell her. "You look like you need a good feed."

Nancy says, "Go get a new plate, girl, have some of mine."

Bill says, "I'll have any leftovers." Of course.

Then it is time for Civics.

"Good afternoon, everybody," says Miss Beech. I am starting to like her. She is quiet and fair. "Today is our first session together for the fascinating, interesting, compulsive Civics Class!"

Everybody laughs at her weak attempt at humour. I look around. There are only twenty-six of us. This is not a popular elective. I am sitting with Rose the Nose, Nancy Drew the Detective girl, and Bill who I refuse to call Retard Taylor. Instead, I am working on a new nickname for him. I'll try Rocky.

Miss Beech has a police officer with her. I thought it was meant to be a fire officer but something must have happened.

"I want you to meet a friend of mine, Officer Benson, who is a police officer and a teacher."

"Good afternoon, all," says Officer Benson. "Please call me Officer Benson."

"Good afternoon, Officer Benson," everyone chants.

Miss Beech continues with her introduction to the class. She tells us what it is about. "Welcome to the Civics Elective. It is an excellent choice because in Civics we can talk and learn about everything, including relationships between boys and girls."

There is a stirring in the class, an awakening of interest.

"The elective is studying and experiencing things that will help keep you safe by helping you make good decisions," she tells the class. "Today and Thursday we are going to learn about how to stay out of harm's way, especially with regard to fire. Officer Benson will be here each lesson to help me and to bring her specialised knowledge to our studies. Officer Benson?"

Officer Benson steps forward. She is a tall lady with wavy fair hair. She has blue eyes and a pretty mouth. She looks more like a fashion model than a police officer. Will she teach us about makeup and stuff? I don't know anything about that.

"I am in my uniform today so you know I am a real police officer. In future sessions I will dress like a teacher. I am with you for the whole term as part of my work in child welfare. I am surprised that schools do not teach much about real life: what to do if you are mugged, how to cope with bullying, what adult behaviour is acceptable, like taking photographs of you if you feel embarrassed."

My stomach lurches. In less than a week I will be twelve and Dad will take nude photos of me for his record of how I change each year. I don't have breasts yet but I feel extremely uncomfortable at the thought of Dad taking photos of my chest.

"Today we will explore fire and what to do if you are involved in one. Miss Beech will sort you into groups and I will give each group a piece of paper for your group's report."

Miss Benson organises six groups of four. We manage to stay together but there is a group of two left over. Miss Benson takes me from my group and puts me with Hayden Millard and one of his goons, the little one. I find the goon's name really is Alan; Alan Pritchard.

"Are you two goons going to apologise to me for your bullying?" I ask.

"Why should we?" says Hayden.

"Because I say so."

"You and whose army?"

"We've had this conversation before and you ended up flat on your back," I tell him.

"Hush everybody," twitters Miss Beech, although it is really only my group making a noise.

We listen to the instructions: we have to list all the possible ways a fire can begin while we are asleep in bed. Next, we have to say what action we would take.

It is quite interesting. Officer Benson takes us to the teachers' car park. She lights a fire in a metal rubbish bin and each group takes a turn to pick up an extinguisher, run to the blaze, but not too close, start the extinguisher and carefully move forward until we can hit the centre of the blaze.

Next, we have a group simulation game where we call Emergency Services. Hayden is the victim. He reads the cue card "Your father's golf cart has caught fire in the garage. Call Emergency Services."

I am the ES officer and Alan is the observer. I tell Hayden he must leave the house immediately. There is no way you can fight a lithium battery fire. Alan says you have to have a plan so everyone in the house can escape without trying to rescue people. I tell them my dad locks me in so we can't escape separately. His door is locked too.

"Your Dad is asking for trouble," says Alan.

He is no longer a bully boy. He is earnestly concerned. "Let me show you how to pick a lock."

I am appalled. I am not a criminal.

Hayden chimes in. He is a different boy when he is giving advice, "Lesley, you'll fry if you don't get out. Your Dad hasn't got time to open your door and his. You heard Officer Benson. The fire sucks all the oxygen within a minute. Listen to Alan. He taught me how to pick a lock. Most of them are as easy as pie."

There is a break halfway through the session. I ask Officer Benson about photos.

"Please Miss Benson, my dad takes nude photos of me on my birthday every year. How can I tell my Dad I am not comfortable now?"

"When is your birthday?"

"Sunday, I'll be twelve."

"Does your father see you undressing, or in the shower?"

"No, Miss. I have my bedroom and en suite. He has his bedroom and the main bathroom. I don't have a Mum."

"What is your name?"

I tell her, "Lesley."

"Well, Lesley, I think you have to tell him tonight that you do not want him to take photos this year. If he is upset and asks why, just say I am a big girl now and I have no Mum. Just that. Don't say any more. Tell me his reaction."

Oh dear. It sounds like I am getting Dad into trouble. "Yes, Miss."

It gets worse. Bill, who I call Rocky but nobody else likes that name, says, "Traitor."

I think he is joking but he is not.

"I couldn't help it." I tell him. "Miss Benson moved me. It could have been you."

"I would not have gone. I would be loyal," he says as he walks off.

Nancy won't look at me. Rose gives me a finger. I've blown it. I now have no friends.

6.

The staff room is empty, surprising for this time of day. Tired teachers at the start of the school year have hurried home, allowing Alison Beech to sink into the most comfortable armchair in the room. The chair is in a bright pocket of sunshine and like a cat, Alison stretches in its warmth. Fiona Benson likes the staff room; unlike the office where she works, this room is a place of rest and restoration. The sun is low and the shadows cast on the pale-yellow wall remind Fiona of prison bars.

Fiona makes the coffee. The machine gurgles and groans and releases two steaming cups of coffee that she carries across the room to her friend, who is lying back with her eyes closed, relaxing after what has been a tiring day

"That went well, Fiona. Are you sure you don't want to come back to teaching?" Alison asks with a friendly smile. "On a day like today, teaching is one of the best jobs in the world."

"No. I love the kids, but the education system is not for me," she replies. "All that paperwork. It's worse than policing. Your Lesley seems to have calmed Hayden Millard down."

Her eyes sparkle with approval for the young girl.

Alison nods, considering the bright student. "She's new. Most of the others know each other from last year, but they are from different classes. I hope that doesn't mean cliques and gangs. Lesley's father mentioned she had private tuition until last year. But every time they move house – and that happens frequently – she gets a new tutor. That explains her lack of social skills. She tells me she had the last one for a couple of years, an older lady who passed away. I think she is still missing her."

Fiona leans in, lowering her voice as if sharing a secret. "She asked me how to tell her dad not to take nude pictures any more."

Regret washes over her the moment the words escape her lips.

"What?" Alison is horrified,

Fiona knows Alison reacts very strongly where men and women are concerned, and makes up her mind she will be the one to deal with the topic of Human Relationships later in the term. "Apparently, he records her on her birthday and at other times throughout the year."

"That's disgusting," says Alison. "I met him on Friday. He stood too close and tried to look down my front. Do you know she has no mother?"

"You hum it, I'll play it," laughs Fiona.

It is an old joke and they both laugh.

Alison Beech says, "We have to report situations where girls might be at risk."

"Oh, Alison. Lesley shows no signs of sexual abuse," Fiona replies. "She was up front about the photo shoots. She had an opportunity to tell me of any problems. I don't see any issues."

"She's on her own with no female adult," Alison says. "That gives him every opportunity to you know what."

"Leave it out, Ali. Right. I'm off," Fiona says before Alison can expand on her fears. "I have a swing shift from six tonight until two in the morning."

The sun has gone. Alison is no longer bathed in sunshine and the prison bar shadows on the yellow wall have gone. The staff room seems to have lost its liveliness and now looks jaded and tired.

Fiona stops in the doorway, looks back at the friend and says, "Alison, you are a worrier. There is no reason to believe something is going on behind closed doors. See you on Thursday."

After Fiona leaves, Alison Beech's mind dwells on what Fiona told her about Lesley with no mother, and with a father who has a job that keeps him away at night. What if there is a fire?

'Poor kid,' she thinks. 'I don't know what is worse, her father neglecting her or her father being home. I don't want to be blamed for not reporting such a difficult situation.'

She comes to a decision and reaches for her mobile phone.

7.

When the class finishes Bill leaves me behind. He doesn't walk me home. I think that is because I worked with Hayden and Alan and because Hayden seems to have a crush on me.

Surprisingly, Alan asks me to go to his house to look at locks and find the kind I've got. I have the time. I'll do my homework after dinner.

As I set off with Alan, Hayden joins us. I look back. Bill is waiting outside for me. Without meaning to, I have made another blunder. Is this why I always lose friends? Bill has his hands on his hips and is glaring at me. I turn my back and walk off.

"I'm not going with you if you bully me," I tell Hayden and Alan. "What's with you anyway? You're good looking, clever, only have one head. I don't get it."

We walk in silence for a while.

Alan says, "People call him dumb."

"Shut up!" roars Hayden.

Dad is right. Find the problem.

"Nobody likes me."

"I do," says Alan. "Me and Rodney."

Rodney is a quiet boy with brown skin. I think his parents might be from Pakistan.

Hayden answers Alan, "Youse guys don't count. You're thicker than me!"

I intervene. "Stop it guys. You are making yourselves victims of other people's bullying."

They shut up and we walk on.

"How come you're so bright?" asks Hayden.

"I listen to my teachers," I reply. "You should try it sometime."

Alan's home is a Council house. It is set back from the street a little way, just enough to get a car in for parking. There is junk everywhere. I look hard at Alan to try to place him in this dump. I notice his school uniform is ragged and too big for his small frame. He has a gaunt look as if he doesn't get enough food. Like me. The gaunt look. I get plenty of food but people think I am anorexic.

We enter the house by climbing through Alan's bedroom window.

"Mum's got the only key. She's at work."

Hayden says, "Are we going to be long? I can pick locks now so I don't need to be here."

So why did he walk with us? Good question.

While Alan sorts though his locks, he has a lot of them, I look around. His room is small; it is a council house. Social housing, we're meant to say. The curtains are shredded. They are old and musty. His bed smells like a dog sleeps in it; a wet dog too. He has clean clothes in a pile at the end of the bed. They are spotless: a vest, a pair of underpants, a too-large shirt that has come from someone else, and a pair of fresh school socks. There is a set of tracksuit pants, small enough to be a girl's but he will fit into them nicely.

Alan takes over. In a bottom drawer he has several locks. I point at the kind on my door.

"Easy," he says, unclicking the lock.

"Doesn't he know about fires?"

Of course Dad knows about fires. The house burned down and all the photos and papers were destroyed. I stop in shock. Did Mum die because he had locked her in?

Alan opens the lock. I won't tell you what he does, nor about the tool he uses. He opens it in five seconds. He closes it in less time.

"Your turn."

I try but I can't undo it. He is a patient teacher. After a few trials, the lock opens. Alan makes me repeat my actions.

"Take the lock home and practise," he says. He gives me the lock.

I leave through the window. I turn left to go home. Bill comes out of a gateway set back in a hedge. Bill looks furtive. If I was looking out of one of the windows facing the street, I would be calling the police.

"What are you doing here?" I ask him. I hold out my hand and he takes it in his; tenderly for a big boy.

"Nothing. Just going for a walk."

Oh yeah?

We walk along together.

"What are you doing here?" he asks.

"Learning how to pick a lock," I tell him. "If there's a fire, I'm toast. Alan taught me to open the lock on my door."

"Why does your dad do that? Lock you in?" asks Bill. "That's crazy."

"It's just my dad. In Latvia the secret police come and take you away. Dad always sits near a window ready to jump out."

I say nothing more to Bill.

We walk on. He says, "Sorry I growled at you. We promised to stick together."

"Yeah, but things happen. I'm back with you now. On Thursday it might be you who has to change groups."

"I hadn't thought of that."

We go past the shop on the corner. The shopkeeper gives me a wave. I like her. I drop Bill's hand and wave back. She is a nice lady; her name is Gladys Tennyson. Her husband drives buses.

"This is my house," I tell him as I stop at the gate. "I can't ask you in. I'm not allowed to ask friends home."

"Why not? Doesn't your father trust you? He's not making drugs, is he?"

"No. He's a good Dad. I suppose he wants to keep me safe."

We say goodbye and Bill leaves. I am left with some significant questions. What is it with Hayden? What is it with Bill? I get Alan. I must check with Rose the Nose about his diet. And the clean clothes.

8.

I have to buy bread and vegetable protein meat substitute for dinner tonight. I'll buy some bread, and milk too. As soon as Bill is out of sight, I turn to go back to the corner shop. I hope the old man next door doesn't want to talk today.

Only two cars pass me as I walk to the corner shop. The old man is not in his garden. I like talking to him but today I haven't got the time. It is a warm afternoon even though it is early Autumn. I see a garden with an apple tree with red and yellow leaves. It looks lovely. Or is it a cherry tree? Anyway, its leaves are beginning to fall.

Even though there isn't much garden, if we can stay in this house I could have a blossom tree, and flowers like the old man grows. If only Dad's job didn't mean shifting from one rented house to another.

The shop looks as if it has been there a thousand years. The shelves against the wall are full of all sorts of things, unlike a supermarket where similar things are all in one place. There is a spicy smell in the air. The groceries are at the back of the shop. That's where I will find the meat substitute. I go down the narrow passage between two rows of shelving.

"Hello neighbour," says a man's voice. "Do you remember me? Sam Bennet?"

"Yes, Mister Bennet. How are you?" I reply in my polite voice.

"Well. Very well. I must come over and meet your Mum and Dad sometime."

"I have no Mum. She was killed in a car crash. Dad works different hours each day but you'll see his car when he is home."

I am not sure I want Mister Bennet to meet Dad. While I am thinking, Mister Bennet says," Well, I've got what I came for. I'll see you later."

It doesn't take me long to find some nice vegetarian mince. I see some potatoes so I buy enough for two meals. Tinned tomatoes are cheap. Milk and bread are at the counter. Mister Bennet is just leaving as I put my basket on the counter.

"The Smith account," I say. Dad has set up a tab. He pays so much every payday and Mrs Tennyson charges that account.

"How are you today, young Lesley?" she asks. At least she doesn't call me Poppet.

"I am fine, thank you Mrs Tennyson."

"Oy. There was a lady asking after you," she said. "Your Dad's cousin, she told me."

I look blankly at Mrs Tennyson. "Dad is an orphan. He has nobody except me," I tell her. "Mum and her parents were killed in a car crash nine years ago."

"She must have the wrong Smith," Mrs Tennyson tells me. "There are lots of Smiths."

"Thank you for telling me. What did she look like?"

"Welfare. She looked like Welfare. I can spot Welfare a mile away. I was in Harrison Hall when I was young. So was my hubby, Terry Tennyson. That's where we met. That was the only good thing about being in Harrison Hall. Ten years I was there. I left the day I turned seventeen and set up with Terry. Take care, Lesley. If she is lying about being John's cousin, she is up to no good."

I say my goodbyes and head home. I see Mister Bennet sitting on the kerb with his head down low.

I run to him and ask. "Mister Bennet? Are you alright?"

"Aye, lass. I tripped on my pull-along cart." He waves at the wheeled bag that holds his groceries. It is lying on the ground upside down. "I fell and hurt my leg. Give us a hand up, please, love."

I put my hand under his elbow and steady him as he gets slowly to his feet.

I check the cart. I stand it upright. It is not heavy; he hasn't bought much. Nothing is leaking. There is no damage I can see. "If I put my bag in your cart, I can pull it home for you."

I don't wait for a reply. I just do it.

Together we walk along the street. Mister Bennet has to stop frequently. He is breathing heavily.

"Mister Bennet, I want you to come in and have a cup of tea. You can relax and get your breath back."

"I'd like that," he says. "I have a cream bun in my cart. We can have half each."

Dad is late. I check my phone. No message. Mister Bennet and I share his cream bun. We talk. He was a veterinarian in the Navy, an animal doctor. He was an officer and he travelled the world. I hadn't known the Navy had so many animals. I knew about horses for parades and stuff but there are dogs and cows and goats and some special animals like monkeys and rats. The rats are used to find landmines and bombs. I must tell Miss Beech about him and ask if he can talk to the Civics class.

It is autumn and the nights are drawing in. It is dark when Mister Bennet leaves. I get a torch to light the way as I see him back to his house.

On the way back I see a silver car on the opposite side of the road. There is an older lady in the car. I give her a wave to let her know I have seen her. If she really is a relative, she will wind down the window to talk to me.

She doesn't.

"Who is that?" he asks.

"Mrs Tennyson thinks she is Welfare," I tell him. "She is spying on me because Dad often leaves me on my own."

He crosses the road and taps on the car's window.

"What are you doing here?" he asks.

I can hear him clearly but I have to strain to hear her.

"Well, there's nowt here needing supervision," he says. "So you can just clear off."

The lady raises her voice. "I have to ensure children are safe. That's my job."

"And I am telling you, you are a busybody who upsets people who see you lurking. There is only one child here and that is Lesley Smith. She is under my care when her dad works late. You have no reason to be here. You are snooping, looking for trouble, so clear off or I will have the Law on you."

Go Mister Bennet!

The woman starts her car. She makes the motor roar as she drives off.

Mister Bennet walks back to me.

"Thank you, Mister Bennet. I am scared she is going to take me away."

"Not any more," he says. "You come to me. I'll look after you. Spying! I'm going to tell the police."

"Goodnight, Mister Bennet. Thanks for the cream bun."

"Goodnight, Lassie."

Ugh. I guess Lassie is better than Poppet but not by much.

9.

Across town, in her flat that is part of a block of flats, Alison Beech is talking to Fiona Benson. Her flat is small, one bedroom, a dinette cum kitchen and a small sitting room. A month ago, Miss Beech asked the landlord for new curtains. The old curtains are stained where a previous tenant's toddler grabbed them with sticky hands while learning to walk. How many tenants ago did that happen?

Nobody really knows because for these flats tenants tend to move on as soon as they find their feet. Alison wants to take the curtains down and wash them but is scared they will fall apart and she will have to pay to replace them.

Fiona thinks the landlord wants Alison to do just that. Alison can be so trusting and naïve. Her rules are black and white, and that is what the friends are discussing.

"Lesley Smith is left alone in the house when her father works at night," says Alison. Her hands always appear to be cold; she tucks them in her pockets if her clothing allows, today she is holding her hot cup of coffee with her hands cupped like a tulip.

"Lesley is twelve in a week's time," says Fiona. "She is quite capable of being on her own. I am more concerned with her father taking nude photographs of her."

As soon as the words were out of her mouth, Fiona regrets her action. She wishes she could pull the words back like writing in a bubble so she can take a rubber and erase her words.

"What?"

Alison's shock bounces around the tiny room.

"Oh, nothing to worry about, dear friend," Fiona says, trying to minimise the damage that might follow from her lack of forethought. "Her father has taken photos of her growing up. Lots of people do that."

"Did you say naked?" Alison's voice drops to a whisper. Her facial muscles are taught showing her stress levels are high.

"Look Alison, I shouldn't have said that. Let me tell you the whole story to put your mind at ease. Since his wife died when Lesley was three, he has taken photos of her, clothed and unclothed. Previously she was a little girl but now she is growing up she feels embarrassed and wants to know how to say I don't want you to do that from now on. I gave her some advice and I will monitor the situation."

"But there is no woman in the house," says Alison. Her voice is full of concern. "He could do anything to her."

Her voice hangs on the word 'anything'.

"Alison, the girl shows no signs that would alarm me. Remember please I am trained in this area. What I will do is ask on Thursday how she got on asking her father to desist. "

"Oh, Fiona; I hope you are right. He stood much too close to me on Friday."

"Of course I am. But I am now running late. I have a swing shift today, six o'clock to two."

Alison sees Fiona out. She makes herself another cup of tea while she considers Fiona's news.

'Poor kid, alone and at the mercy of a man,' she tells herself. "I have to do something."

She reaches for her mobile phone and searches for the number of the local Welfare office. She is directed to a non-government agency where she speaks to a Miss Marston.

10.

Dad is tired when he arrives home. I have dinner ready, vegetarian mince patties with tinned tomatoes and cabbage and mashed potato. There is ice cream in the freezer if we want it. We don't.

I clear the table and wash the dishes. Dad dries while I wash. Then I make a pot of tea and we sit in the lounge. This is a suitable time to talk about photographs.

"Dad, it's my birthday on Sunday. I am a big girl now and I have no Mum. I don't want you to take photos of me any more."

Dad is silent for a few minutes. Officer Benson said to say nothing more. I sip my tea.

"Lesley, photos of you growing up are important for me. I have whole collection from when you were three. That was when your mother got killed and the house burned down. You are not grown-up yet so why should I stop?"

Oh boy, what do I do?

" I am a big girl now. I have no Mum. I don't want you to take any more photos of me with no clothes on."

"What brought this about?"

"I am growing up and my body is beginning to change. I feel embarrassed, even when I am wearing clothes. Please, Dad, don't take any more."

"We'll see," he says.

That means he will have to force me and he won't do that. He's a good dad.

"Dad, tell me about my grandparents. We have to make family trees at school and I don't know who my grandparents are."

"Stop right there, Lesley. I don't want the school prying into my family business. Is this shyness about your body coming from the school? I think I had better get another home tutor."

It is all going wrong. Dad is angry, really mad. He might start talking about taking me out of school. I don't want that.

He stands up suddenly. His face is red and puffed up. He is angry. I want to say everything is alright but Officer Benson said just keep things simple. He slaps his cup on the small table and stamps off, really stamps, thump, thump, thump, slam. Thump, thump on the stairs, then the slam of his bedroom door.

I am upset. Shaking. Why is he so angry? Don't take pictures I don't want. Who are my grandparents? What is so terrible about that?

I wash our cups. I dry them. I put out breakfast plates, spoons and two boxes of cereal, I move mechanically. I feel upset and helpless. I go to my room. Dad has left the door unlocked. I don't know if he will come into the room before he locks it so I can't practise undoing the lock Alan Pritchard has given me. I hide the big square lock in the drawer with my pullovers.

I get into bed and read a book.

Dad knocks the opens the door.

"Ready for bed, Poppet?"

"Sorry to upset you, Dad."

"We'll sort it out, Poppet. About your grandparents. You never met your grandparents because two of them died in the house fire after your mother Ann's death in a car accident. My parents abandoned me to an orphanage as a child. I don't know the names of my parents. I was called Markus Johanson by the orphanage in the Crimea. I changed that to Markus Vasiljefs in Latvia. In England I changed my name to John Smith so I couldn't be found.

Your Mum's Grandparents' name was Jones. William and Mary. The house fire destroyed all the papers, photographs, everything. That's why I am obsessive about keeping photos of you. Night, night.

No kiss on my brow. He closes the door and locks it.

11.

As soon as I hear Dad lock his door I start working on my door. Alan's practice lock is similar but different. Dad had a carpenter fit new locks on all the outside doors plus the bathroom and the bedroom doors when we moved in. Our locks are more solid than Alan's practice lock.

I can't open it. I struggle and try again and again. I still can't open it. I'll have to talk to Alan. Tomorrow is Saturday. I might walk to his place if Dad gets busy on something. Sunday is my birthday.

I have not seen the photos Dad took on each birthday. He always shows me one where I have a nice smile. I used to enjoy it; I enjoy everything that makes Dad happy. But why does he take photos of me with no clothes on?

Embarrassing.

I am not letting Dad take photos of me with no clothes.

I go to bed and dream how to make the lock open.

Then in my dream I see the angle of Alan's fingers and I know what to do. It is so late I think it might be tomorrow. The house is quiet. I always have a torch with me in case of power cuts or emergencies. I hold the torch high with one hand and work on the lock with the other. Click. Click. Open. I ease the door open, then close it quietly as I practise locking it. Click. Click, Closed.

I almost jump with joy. Now if there is a fire I can escape.

I am thirsty. I use my torch as I tiptoe to the kitchen, the stairs creaking as I tread on them. I move my feet to the far side where there is more support for the tread. Silence.

The rooms are dark. My torch throws long shadows onto the walls. I can imagine the shadows are animals lurking, waiting for me to come close. I shiver and reach my room without being jumped on.

I am hyper. I feel awesome. I am not a prisoner any more.

What?

I am not a prisoner any more. That came from somewhere inside my brain, hidden from sight because I don't want to feel like that. But it is true. I realise I have been feeling like I am in a prison, not allowed out and not allowed to have people in. Bill, Rose, Nancy Drew, Alan, even Hayden are not totally free because they are still kids but they can come and go as they please within reason They are not locked in their bedrooms at night. Why am I?

This needs some thought.

12.

Someone else is awake in the early hours. Officer Fiona Benson wakes up from a deep sleep. Something is worrying her. She goes over her caseload. She thinks of her Court cases coming up. Finally, she thinks of her work with Alison Beech.

Fiona is thirty-three, Alison is twenty-six, seven years younger. They helped each other through a difficult period of their lives. They met while working in a high school and became friends. Alison was starting her teaching career and was struggling to control her classes.

At that time Fiona was going through a messy and distressing end to a relationship that she thought was her forever love. Things started to decline when she became pregnant and came to a head when she lost her baby. Daniel was not sympathetic. He said having kids was not his idea of fun, it wasn't his idea in the first place.

"It's just as well you miscarried," Daniel told her cruelly. A baby would have ruined everything."

The consequent rows and quarrels and the pressure of the classroom led to a change of lifestyle. Fiona went to Police College and Eric disappeared from her life and Alison found her career in a lowly regarded school in a depressed area of the city where working parents or one parent families had no pretensions. If the teacher said their child misbehaved then that was accepted regardless of the dramatic performances of the offspring.

Fiona proposed assisting with the elective programme. Her inspector thought it was a great idea to reach out to children before they became junior criminals. Now the programme was in its second year and students came to Alison and Fiona for advice, or just to sort things out in this complicated world between childhood and adulthood.

Fiona suddenly sees what is worrying her. The new girl, Lesley. Her Dad wants to take birthday photos of her with no clothes on. Lots of parents take pictures of their children on their birthdays. With Lesley there is something else behind her request. She is to tell her dad that she doesn't want photos taken this year as she is growing up. What is happening? Did the girl follow instructions and just keep to NO? Or did she get involved so he could sweet talk or boss her?

Fiona makes up her mind to ask Alison Beech to check with Lesley on Monday.

13.

I am sitting in the sun in the small garden at the back of our house. The new house is so close I can hear the people talking. I don't want them to think I am snooping but this is my garden and I want to enjoy the sunshine.

I have a good book that I am reading. It's about a boy who looks after flamingos. The Germans come and smash his circus ride. I read until my eyes are tired from the sun. It is going down now and it is time for me to get tea.

I am busy when Dad gets home.

"Hi, Lesley. How are things?"

Lesley? Not Poppet? I am surprised; Dad is getting the message. I am even more surprised as we eat our dinner.

"Have you told your friends about your birthday?" he asks.

"Not really," I say, wondering what is coming next. "It's not on a school day."

"Would you like to go to McDonald's with your friends on Sunday?"

What?

"McDonald's?"

"Yes. With no Mum, you can't really have a birthday party at home. Don't McDonald's have a birthday programme?"

Yes they do! Last year some of the kids in my class raved over their McDonald's parties.

"How many friends have you got?"

"There's Nancy Drew, Rose Knowles, Bill Taylor, Alan Pritchard and Hayden Millard."

"That would be six in total. Let me phone the manager of the McDonald's down town."

He tells the manager I will drop by to choose a birthday package. I head there immediately.

I invite Bill, Alan, Hayden (you behave yourself Hayden), Rose and Nancy Drew, using my phone. I am thrilled that they can all come. I tell them, "No presents, by order."

Sunday begins with a card and a smart phone. Until now I have not been allowed more than a basic email phone.

"Now you are growing up, you should have enough sense to stay safe," he says. "You are not a child any more. But you still must be very cautious."

I give him a kiss that says thank you.

Dad asks if he may take a head and shoulders photo of me in my school uniform. I agree immediately. I can see no harm in that.

Now everything goes slowly. I can hardly wait for two o'clock. I keep checking my phone for the time. I have to check the phone is still working because I keep thinking the clock has stopped.

At one o'clock Rose Nose PMs me. "All OK?"

"What's the time, Rose?"

My clock is right. It is one o'clock. I am so excited. I am so nervous I keep running to the toilet.

"Time to shower," says Dad.

As I leave the shower, I check myself out in my bedroom mirror. I am too grown-up for photos with no clothes on.

I put on my prettiest green frock; it goes beautifully with my red hair. I am bigger. It is tight across the chest and the sleeves, but they are short so they won't matter. I must remember not to stretch my shoulders, to stay upright. I'll talk to Dad about seeing a dressmaker to let the dress out a little; should have thought of that before now.

Dad drives me to McDonald's. We pick up the kids as we go. Alan is on the street, waiting. We have to toot Hayden. Six in the car will be two too many. We are squashed with four. I use my phone. Mrs Drew says she will bring Nancy and Bill.

The party is awesome. The activities are designed for kids our age. They are not stupid games for little kids. We have party hats that look grown up; mine is like the nineteen twenties, a cloche hat? Alan has a spiv's hat.

Uho. Bill pushes Hayden when Hayden wants to sit beside me. I resolve the situation by sitting with Alan on one side and Rose on the other. Nancy Drew catches on and sits between Hayden and Bill. She rather fancies Hayden. Bill fancies Nancy Drew. Kids.

The food is awesome. We get to choose from three things. Alan asks for seconds, and gets them! How he fits two giant burgers into his small body I don't know.

The event is a great success; the first actual party I have had, the first time I have been the centre of attention, and the first time I have had boys fighting over me. Well, not quite fighting but nearly.

After the party I am buzzing. Dad is pleased for me.

"I hope you have some room left," he says. "I've ordered Chinese for dinner."

Chinese takeaway is a special treat. It is delivered right on seven o'clock. Any earlier and I could not have eaten it. I love the dim sims. I am not hungry but I eat six of them! Awesome.

It's been a great day. McDonalds AND Chinese in one day! Wow!

Dad and I watch some telly. I thank him again for the party.

"Thanks Dad. Today has been so special."

"I am pleased for you," says Dad. "Are you growing out of your best dress?"

"It is tight, Dad. A dressmaker can let it out."

"No, Lesley. The dress is beautiful but I think you need one more suited to your age. Where is the best young lady's shop?"

"I'll ask around, Dad. Thank you."

It seems to be the perfect day. Awesome.

While I am having my party, I think about Officer Fiona Benson. She is a lovely lady; she is not only beautiful; she is also very caring. Perhaps I should have asked her and Miss Beech to McDonald's.

No. That's a terrible idea.

14.

Fiona Benson has a shower to wash off the stress of a heavy day. Sunday has brought problem after problem. Especially domestics. It's always the kids who suffer from domestic disputes. It's always the female officers who get to deal with them.

She has a bruise on her arm where an angry man grabbed her and pushed her away from protecting his wife. She grabbed his wrist and pulled his arm up his back. She held him until he had calmed down. Greta, the officer with her, dealt with the wife when she saw Fiona had the situation under control. When the man went limp. Fiona released his arm and talked quietly to him.

Graham Hill is a fire officer. Fiona talks to him about self-control and assessing the needs of a situation. He calms down. Officer Greta Green and wife Julie Hill have gone into a bedroom. The kids come out to see what is happening. They are three little girls. They sit on the sofa in order of their height. Sweet.

"I lost my rag," he admits. "Greta doesn't understand how tired I get. When I get in, she just wants me to take her to the pub to have a good time."

"Officer Green will deal with that," Fiona tells him. "Graham Hill, I ought to ticket you for assaulting an officer. I'll forgive you once, because you calmed down quickly. Next time you lose your rag, leave it. Walk off. At work, at home, it doesn't matter. Just walk away. Leave it."

Now, at home, Fiona pours a white wine. Time to relax.

The phone rings. Alison Beech is calling. Fiona answers the phone.

"Oh hi, Alison. What news?

"Hi Fee. I'm a bit worried about Lesley Smith. She seems to be spending too much time with the unruly boys. She is really a very anxious child."

"Don't worry about those boys, Ali. She seems able to control them better than I can. Isn't her birthday this weekend?"

"Today."

"Could you check her out tomorrow? Ask how the birthday went? Be careful about photographs; you are not meant to know that she confided in me. You could ask if anyone took photos on her birthday and can you see them. If she had a party, the kids would have taken oodles."

"She is so genuine."

"Or ingenuous. I like that girl."

Fiona suddenly realises that she has strong protective feelings for Lesley. She is a special girl.

'My baby would be her age by now,' she thinks. 'If I ever have a kid, I hope she is like Lesley. Knowing my luck, it will be a boy like Hayden!"

She laughs and settles down with her wine.

She returns to her thoughts on Lesley. 'Is it just an empty yearning for someone to fill my baby's place? Or have we so much I common we have an almost mother-daughter relationship? Are adults, especially a warranted officer, allowed to fall in love with a child and pray the child can one day be hers?'

15.

Later in the night, I wake up with a stomach ache.

"Too much shop-bought food. McDonalds and Chinese, what a day."

I think I hear a telephone conversation. Unlocking my door I creep outside Dad's door. I hear Dad say, "Lesley will not have her photo taken nude now she is growing up. "

I can hear a man's voice replying but cannot hear what is being said. The man is aggressive. Dad is trying to calm him.

"It's alright, Eric. We can start the video with her in a school uniform then use last year's photos of her buck naked."

Video? Dad was making videos of me? not just taking photos?

I hear the man on the phone giving a sharp reply.

I hear my father say, "Get rid of her? That needs thought."

There is a quieter reply, then Dad says, "That new little girl you've found. I'll need to change towns and get rid of Lesley before you snatch her."

The man called Eric speaks in a calmer voice,

Dad's reply is something like, "It's all very well for you to say, you've never had to get rid of someone."

There is a short comment.

"I don't know yet. At the moment she suspects nothing but she is not going to be happy about changing schools, I can tell you."

There is a scraping of a chair on the floor. I high tail it back to my room and lock myself in. The lock makes a loud click. I lie in bed dreading Dad charging in. I lie awake for most of the night.

16.

I am used to walking to school now. I sometimes meet the two ladies with the baby in its pram. They are mother and daughter. Hayden and his gang avoid the park. They know I will challenge them. The weekend was magic. I can't thank Dad enough. It's a shame weekends can't go on forever.

Because of the telephone call I overheard, I didn't get much sleep. On Friday, Miss Beech set us homework, "Find photos of you as a baby. We will share them on Monday."

That is right now. I don't have any baby photos. I hope Miss Beech doesn't notice.

She walks around the room. There are eight groups. She sees I have no baby photos. My earliest photos are from when I was four.

"Lesley, did you forget to do your homework?" she asks. "Or did you get muddled?"

"No Miss Beech. Dad has no baby photos of me. I don't have any grandparents. My Dad is an orphan and both Mum and her parents are dead."

Miss Beech is surprised.

I hope to make her lose her focus by chattering. "He took some lovely photos of me in my uniform and of my face. He is getting them printed and framed. And he gave me a smart phone but I don't know how to use it yet."

I need to see Miss Beech privately. She is busy but I catch her at the morning break.

"Miss, I'm worried about my Dad and his photographs. I think he is trying to get rid of me."

"Lesley, your father is checked by the police every year because he is a crane driver. Tell me about the photos he took on your birthday."

"They are not the ones, Miss. It's the ones without clothes on I am worried about."

"From your last birthday?"

"Not only then but through the year as well."

"Lesley, if nothing bad has happened in an entire year, nothing will happen now. I think you have worked yourself up into a state of anxiety. You look tired. I think you will see things differently after a good sleep so run along now but keep me informed."

I hadn't expected that. Miss Beech treating me like a seven-year-old. Officer Benson will be at Civics tomorrow afternoon. I'll tell her. But without evidence will she believe me? No. And that is too late.

I could be dead by then.

This is really serious stuff. I'll have to go into Dad's room after school and find something to show Officer Benson, maybe a scribbled note with a name or something on it. Then I'll have to stick it out until tomorrow.

"Hi Gloomy." It is Bill, with a soppy grin on his face. "Where's your boyfriend?"

That annoys me.

"If you mean Hayden, I have no idea. I don't have a boyfriend. I have three boys who are my friends. You are one of them. Actually, you are the one I like the most."

Bill is completely honest. I trust him. Will he laugh at me?

I decide to test him to see if he can keep a secret. "How long can you keep a secret?" Trick question. 'Forever' means they are lying.

"It depends if someone is going to get hurt or cheated or whatever. Sometimes things happen that mean you should tell a secret but usually I keep a secret until it isn't any more."

Good answer.

"Bill, I need a good friend. I need someone who can keep a secret until it is time to tell. I need some advice."

"Okay. That's me."

"I think my Dad is going to kill me."

"I won't keep that a secret. Tell Miss Beech."

"I tried to but she said I had worked myself into a state of anxiety. That means I am imagining things."

"What makes you think your dad wants to kill you?"

"He was on the phone late at night. I went to the kitchen for bicarbonate of soda for a stomach ache. I heard him say something like if you've found a new child, I have to get rid of Lesley before I can take her.'"

"What about Officer Benson? We have her tomorrow afternoon. Can you get through till then, Lesley?"

"What would you do, Bill?"

Bill's mouth is open. While Bill thinks for a moment, I add something more. "He said, 'It's all very well for you, you've never had to get rid of someone.'"

His mouth closes but his jaw works as if he is chewing something. Then he speaks. "I'd like to look around his room, find a note or photos or something. Listen, can you include the others in this?"

"Not yet Bill. Let's find some evidence first. I want to tell Officer Benson tomorrow. We'll go into Dad's office after school."

"No. Let's skip school and go now."

17.

Bill and I skip school. It's all very well to say, 'Let's skip school' but you have to collect stuff from your locker, walk down the corridor, leave through the doors and walk along the driveway beside the class room windows. Everyone can see you. And we are a boy and a girl and people think we are boyfriend and girlfriend. Embarrassing.

It is so important we have to go through with it. There is a list about when you can break rules. I am sure trying to save your life is on it. I have a sick feeling from a guilty conscience. I have been at a proper school for less than a year. I have not had a day off, let alone played truant.

"Bill, we'll be in big trouble," I tell him.

"We have a good reason," says Bill. "If we are quick, we can get back to school before classes finish."

In the afternoons we have different teachers for some subjects. This afternoon it is Miss Beech for Social Studies. That is not so bad. Mister Tucker for Science would be a disaster.

I feel people staring as we walk through the park. Just as well the two ladies and the baby aren't here. I rush past the shop. Mister Bennet is not outside. I get my key ready for a quick entrance.

We both feel guilty as we slip through the front door. I feel even more shame because I promised not to bring anyone home from school, let alone a boy on his own. Bill is putting on a brave face but he is edgy.

We go upstairs to the bedrooms. This is getting worse and worse.

"Come on, hurry up and get the door open," he says as I fiddle with the lock on Dad's bedroom door.

"Hang on, you can't hurry this," I tell him.

There is a click from the lock. Bill turns the handle and swings the door open.

The room is tidy. There are no papers on the tabletop. Bill goes to the wastepaper bin. It is empty. The answerphone is empty. There is no evidence of any wrongdoing.

Bill tries the drawers. They are locked. I quickly unlock them. I'm getting good at this. There are four drawers, two on each side. I can hardly breathe. My chest is tight and I am holding my breath. Bill is all fingers and thumbs. There are folders in the top drawer on the right. They are about operating several types of cranes. There is blank paper for the printer. I try the top drawer on the left. There is a two-way dictionary, Latvian and English.

The last drawer is sticky. Bill has to give a strong pull. The whole drawer pops outs. Papers spill on the floor. They are printed photographs. Dad has taken photographs while working. They are excellent shots from up high in the crane. Some show what is below. Others show the wider scenery. One picture is of a woman putting on her bra, forgetting she is beside an open window.

"This is hopeless," says Bill. "Let's tidy up and head off."

Under the papers I see a red memory stick.

"Have you got a computer, Bill?"

"There's one in the school library we can use," he says. "Let's put everything back and go."

There is a great deal of tension as we imagine Dad walking in on us. Our haste to get out makes us careless: I forget to lock the drawers.

We hurry back to school. We are in luck; the library has no class in it. The computer is available. I can operate a computer but feel uneasy. Bill takes over, loads the memory stick and waits.

He is asked for a password.

We try various words but have to admit defeat. We hurry to the Civics class.

We make a mistake by slipping into the classroom together, which causes an enormous "Woohoo!"

Miss Beech says," Bill and Lesley, please see me at the end of class."

There is another "Woohoo!"

"Loser," says Hayden. "We know what you've been doing."

My face is as red as a beetroot.

"Shut up Hayden," says Rose.

Hayden pinches the muscle of her upper arm. Rose is badly hurt but refuses to show it. Nancy Drew puts a foot behind Hayden's legs and pushes him. He crashes over.

"Outside, you two," says Miss Beech.

"She tripped me, Miss," whines Hayden.

"Out."

Both leave the room. There is total silence. Nobody makes a sound while Miss Beech is away.

Miss Beech returns from taking Nancy and Hayden to the Office.

"Right class. Pack up and leave. It's ten minutes early but there's no point in sitting around. You two, wait."

The class leaves silently.

"Explain your behaviour." Miss Beech is firm and strict. "Bill, you first. Lesley, wait outside."

I wait outside in the corridor. This is as bad as walking home; everyone stares. Some smile knowingly; some make smart comments. It is a lonely and embarrassing five minutes. Eventually the door opens and Bill says, "Your turn."

Miss Beech does not react as I had expected.

"Lesley, you came to me this morning and said you were worried about your father's photographs. I cut you short because I was busy. Tell me what happened next."

"Miss, I overheard a telephone conversation between Dad and a man called Eric. I could only hear one side, but I could hear Eric's voice. He is a foreigner. Dad said about using the video and pictures of me in my school uniform and earlier videos of me naked. He said he has found another girl; she is about three, and Dad has to change towns and he has to get rid of me."

My burning face turns white as I speak. I start to shiver.

Miss Beech takes both my hands.

"My dear, you are in shock. I need to talk to Officer Benson. She was here for a few minutes but left just before you came to class. Now, will your father find out you have been in his room?"

I think for a few seconds. "No, Miss Beech. I am sure I locked his door but I will check when I get home."

"Have you anywhere you could stay for the night?"

"No, Miss. That would make Dad suspicious."

Miss Beech asks Bill to come and join us. She holds out her phone. "Here is my number. Phone me in an emergency."

Bill puts the number in his contacts. I try to but can't do Contacts yet.

"I'll text it to you," says Bill.

"I will take the memory stick to Officer Benson and she will have people who can open it. Then we will see what happens. Okay with that?"

No. But what can we do about it?

Nothing.

But Miss Beech is right. There is no reason for Dad to find out we have been in his room. And we have her phone number.

18.

I really expected better of Miss Beech. She doesn't get it. She thinks we are kids with big imaginations. As we leave the school, we should be grateful that we are not on detention, or worse, stood down. How would I explain that to Dad? The school that I am growing to love today seems cold and grey, as unhelpful as a block of concrete, which I guess it is in reality.

I felt I had a right to be taken as an adult and was treated as a seven-year-old. 'Run along now and phone me if you need help.' My life might not be in danger but my fear should have been taken as real. It was so real: I have seen Dad explode at times. I have seen him scared to open the door. I know he believes paid assassins are going to kill him.

Bill is speechless as we leave Miss Beech. As we walk home, he opens up.

"Lesley, Miss Beech was hopeless. She has left you in danger. You'll have to run away."

Oh, how I wish I could. Dad is my father; I have dubbed him in to the police. Well, Miss Beech who will tell Officer Benson. My own father. I can't believe I did that.

"You can come to my house. Mum will understand but I think Dad wouldn't want to get involved with a runaway girl."

Bill means well but he just doesn't get it. I have just ruined my life. If Dad goes to prison, I will be an orphan, sort of. I will end up in Welfare or a foster home. I am not old enough to get by on my own. I mustn't cry. Dad will notice. He will go ape. Maybe even hit me, which he has never done.

"I'll set up a watch," says Bill. "I'll watch your house all night."

I don't know how he expects to do that. He is twelve, The same as me. I wish Officer Benson had still been at Civics.

"Let's go to the Police Station," I say. "I need Officer Benson."

We detour. We walk past Alan's house. Alan and Hayden are playing some game like Cops and Robbers around the building. Hayden is hiding behind a broken-down car, shooting at Alan with his fingers.

"Hey, Pritchard, Millard," yells Bill.

They stop shooting at each other with finger pistols and come to the fence.

Bill says, "I want you to help Lesley. If her Dad finds we have stolen something from his room he might hurt her really bad. We need to keep watch until he goes to bed."

"What time is that?" asks Hayden, looking at me,

"About ten thirty."

"I think I can help," says Alan. "I'll tell Mum I'm at Hayden's".

"When will he get home?" asks Hayden with concern in his voice. "Why don't you just give back what you've stolen?"

"Miss Beech has it," I tell him. "It's a memory stick. I can get it back tomorrow."

I hope.

The boys arrange to hang around from after tea until ten thirty. I don't want them to keep watch but it is a kind gesture. I don't know what they can do if Dad turns nasty but I guess they'll think of something, maybe get Bill's dad to come and knock on the door.

"Thanks guys. I would prefer to set my phone ready to call Bill who can get his dad to help."

"And us," says Alan. For a small guy he's got some guts. The guys agree. I know Bill will confide in his Dad and that is my best bet.

Bill walks me home. He squeezes my hand as he says goodbye.

"I'll be back later," he says. "We will keep an eye on the house until your Dad goes to bed. If there is any trouble, scream and try to run outside. Stay calm and probably nothing bad will happen, but if it does, you won't be on your own."

He is right. Nobody in their right mind would kill you if there was a witness present. It never occurred to me that he might kill the witness. That is not a possibility.

19.

In another part of town, a man parks his car around a corner and walks back to Sally's house. He has been here before. He has watched the little girl from a distance. He has spoken to her twice. A week ago, he took her for a walk while she rode on her trike. She is there, riding around and around the lawn.

"Hello," he says. "Shall we go for another walk?"

The man is kind. He has spoken to her several times and took her for a walk. She feels she can trust him.

"Yeth, pleath."

"Look, I have to go, but after you have had your bath and your tea, I'll take you for a walk before you have go to bed."

"Alright."

"Alright, what?"

"Alright thank you.""

He leaves the little girl. He keeps the house under observation, waiting for the girl to reappear for her ride.

"Hello Mithter Grandad."

She is damp and pink and smells of shampoo.

"Mummy made me have my bath before I ride my trike."

"Where is your daddy?"

"Mummy theth he hath gone away."

"Then I will be your Daddy. Is that good?"

"Mmmm. Yeth. Thank you, Mithter Daddy."

"Come on then, we'll go to the park. Would you like that?"

He opens the gate and they go off together, a father and his little girl enjoying a stroll before bed.

20.

I feel lonely after Bill leaves, so I go to see Mister Bennet. Now I know him, I can visit him at home. I chat with him. We play cards until six o'clock, then it is time for me to get dinner. He walks me back to my house.

"Do you want me to come in and keep you company for a while?" he asks. "You seem to be quite on edge tonight."

I make him a cup of tea. I have Milo. We watch the news channel

"Well, I'll be off," he says. "You do know you can come to me any time you feel unsafe, don't you? You know where I keep the key."

It is a kind offer. My eyes water as I say, "Yes, thank you Mister Bennet. Dad will be here soon."

He leaves me. I am a nervous wreck. I know I wear my lies on my face. That's why I always tell the truth. I am feeling bad about having to deceive my father.

He has treated me well, even lovingly. I love him and cannot believe what I know to be true. Is this the way I pay him back?

But is he really my father?

I have had some doubts, mainly because I cannot check what he has told me.

My mother dying in a car crash? Dad has always been vague and fudged details so I could not find a report of some kind, not even a Coroner's Report.

No grandparents. I believed him when he said he was an orphan, but is he? Is that an excuse so nobody knows his connections?

What about the convenient deaths of Mum's parents at the same time as Mum died.? I am feeling confused about John Smith. I want to confront him, challenge him, but at the same time I want to believe him.

Except he told Eric he has to get rid of me before he can take a new child.

Get rid of me? If Dad doesn't do it, Eric will get rid of me. He seems to control Dad. I wonder if he is an active part of the gang Dad fears so much? Keeping Dad in line, making him earn money for them?

On balance, my head says he is not my Dad while my heart says he is a brilliant dad.

Miss Beech, you just don't get it.

I open the door. It is almost dark outside. I feel a warmth and calmness when I think of my new friends. I've never had friends before. Not like these. I did not want the girls involved but they are and I am grateful. Dad surely won't hurt the girls.

Rose has done the first shift and gone home. She has been replaced by Nancy Drew, who has her bicycle. She is outside the house next door and seems to be working on her chain. Every now and then she pretends to use her phone. I laugh at her act. All it needs is for some poor man to offer to help her fix the bike.

It is beginning to get a little darker. Nancy Drew waves to me before riding home. I cannot see Alan. I know he is there. Somewhere. Alan is so dependable.

Hurry up, Dad. I want to get to bed behind a locked door.

He won't be able to open it if I use the house key to block the hole from the inside. If Dad comes for me; that will buy me enough time to use my phone. The Watch can knock on the door and ring for help. Brilliant.

Dad is very late. What if his way of getting rid of me is to abandon me? Or drown me as if it is an accident. Lock me in and set fire to the house. Or get Eric to. I am ready for that, thanks to Alan.

21.

While I am feeling sick and wondering what to do, I think of the problems Miss Beech has caused by treating me like a ten-year-old. I wonder what she is doing right at this minute.

Right at this minute, Miss Beech is worrying. She puts down the book she is trying to read. Her mind keeps wandering off to her work at school. Education is not just about passing on knowledge. It involves creating relationships of trust and respect.

She knows she has lost the respect of Lesley Smith. Bill Taylor's disgust was written all over his face. Miss Beech doesn't know what to do. She should have listened to Lesley.

She has the red memory stick. That is what is bothering her, an unfulfilled promise. She promised she would give it to Fiona Benson and forgot.

It still might be kids getting wound up. It might be just a child's anxiety, a childish game gone wrong. But Lesley was so sincere. She has probably never told a lie in her entire life. But Lesley must have believed the matter was extremely serious because she skipped Social Studies to find evidence. She thought of a maxim from her training, decide not on what people say but on what they do.

Alarm bells should have rung.

It gets worse. Too late now.

The phone rings. "Alison Beech. How may I help?"

"Miss Beech, I am Bill, Bill Taylor. Sorry to bother you but we think Lesley is going to be hurt or even killed by her father. We couldn't get any help and Miss Benson wasn't available so we are keeping watch on Lesley's house ourselves in case something awful happens. It's because of the red memory stick."

Alison's stomach lurches. The red memory stick. She said the girl had no evidence. Of course, if there was something nasty happening, it would be on the stick, and Mister Smith would do anything to get it back. If Lesley said her teacher has the red memory stick, Mister Smith might get angry but surely he wouldn't hurt her. He seemed such a nice man when she met him. What did Lesley say, "He wants to dispose of me." Surely, she is exaggerating.

Bill's voice continues. "There has been a noise like crockery being thrown or smashed, a lot of shouting by Mister Smith, stamping and yelling. Could you please get Miss Benson to come and help us? We don't want to call the police because if it is just an accident Mister Smith will be very angry."

Miss Beech calls Officer Benson.

"Hi Alison. It's late for you to call. I finished my shift an hour ago, grabbed a burger, showered and now I'm going to bed."

"I've made a blunder, Fiona. This time it is a serious issue. Lesley Smith came to me with a story of stealing her father's memory stick because that will have the evidence, I told her she needed for me to take her seriously. She says her father is going to get another child and dispose of Lesley. It sounded like over anxiety to me. I took the memory stick and said I would give it to you."

Officer Benson's instincts take over. With the phone on speaker, she begins to change back into her uniform. She also changes back to police mode.

"Alison, get to the point. Why ring me now?"

"The kids were so worried for Lesley's safety they arranged a night watch. Bill Taylor rang me to say he needs adult help at Lesley's house. He thinks she is being beaten up."

"What did you take from the words 'disposed of'?"

"Well, got rid of, thrown away."

"And you didn't think that was serious enough to do something about? Why didn't you call me?"

"Well, I didn't want to make a fuss."

"Alison, you are going to have to buy some Big Girl pants. You are a teacher in charge of thirty students for God's sake. If the father is selling pornographic photos of children, or worse, what do you think he might do to dispose of her? Tell her not to do it again? Sell her on the sex market? Lock her in her room and burn the house down?"

Alison is crying. Fiona has gone too far.

"Alison, listen. Bill Taylor phoned you so you have his number. Text it to me. Now. Then get in your car and take that USB stick to my station. Insist that you are under my orders, and the contents are to be treated as evidence of a serious crime."

Alison Beech goes cold and calm. "Bill's number. Here it is."

She sends the number by text. She is now her professional self.

"Got it," says Officer Fiona Benson. "You sound calmer now, Alison. Can you get that memory stick to the station?"

"On it now. Call me when you can."

22.

"Evening Poppet," sings Dad's voice as he opens the door. "Sorry to be so late."

"I was getting worried about you," I say, giving him my usual hug. "I've kept some sausages for you. I'll do you some eggs and chips and reheat your baked beans."

Dad makes no comment about why he is late. We have a silent time while Dad washes up. He gets quite sweaty in his job, and he likes to freshen up. The air fryer quickly reheats the French fries I cooked earlier. I give them an extra minute to make them crisp and brown.

Dad comes down the stairs. His face is tight. He looks as if he has seen a burglar.

"What's wrong Dad?"

I should be frightened but I am not.

His face is a purple colour. His eyes are round and wild. He seems to be holding his breath.

"Dad! Whatever's got into you?"

He lets his breath go and shouts, "You've been in my room! How did you get in? Who else was with you?"

He stamps his way to the table, picks up the plate of food I have set down for him and dashes it on the table. The plate splinters and hot sausages, chips, baked beans and eggs spew everywhere.

I look at him calmly. I can't believe how good an actor I am. Me, who never lies because it shows on my face.

"You left your door unlocked. I went in to tidy up. There was a drawer partly open. I pulled it and papers spilled over the floor. I tidied around but I didn't need to do much, just a little dusting."

Dad's mouth hangs open. He is speechless. He stands still, eyes closed, breathing heavily.

I wait.

He turns away from me.

"I've already eaten," he says. I hear stamp. stamp, stamp all the way across the room, up the stairs and then SLAM goes his door.

With a sigh and a sinking feeling that Dad hasn't finished yet, I clean up the mess. I guess I have blown it. He has to kill me now.

I feel sick.

My life with Dad is over.

The boys are on watch. With all the noise and the tension, they will be wondering if I'm still alive. I sing a song. 'We Are the Champions'. Queen. An old one but a good one. I can sing it loudly, over and over.

23.

The rain sweeps in on a broom of cold wind. Autumn rain is needed for the garden and the grass in the parks but it is cold and wet for the watchers.

Outside the house, Bill is waiting for Miss Beech to come. He sees Mister Smith park his car and walk up the path to the house, which is set a little higher than the road. Bill sneaks up the path so he can listen at the door.

At first, he hears nothing except Lesley moving in the kitchen. She is making normal noises and there is no talk. He stays by the door. He reviews what has happened, turning ideas over in his mind to make sure he has got things right. Have we over-reacted? How serious is the threat to Lesley? He thinks that on balance, we have got it right. All we are doing is keeping watch. If things get bad, I can call for help.

He hears smashing china, shouting, angry steps. He hears Lesley answer calmly. Then he hears stamping footsteps, a slam of an upstairs door. Then there is silence.

Bill doesn't know what to do. He waits, listening for any sound that will give him a clue. Lesley begins singing. She is alright but what if her father comes downstairs and attacks her?

A twelve-year-old can't restrain a grown man but four kids might.

His phone is in his hand. He rings Rose and Nancy Drew. "Help me please." He leaves a message on Hayden's phone.

Outside, as rain begins to fall, Bill is feeling miserable. What can a kid do if a man wants to murder his daughter? It would be all over before he got into the house, assuming the door isn't locked.

Then what? A twelve-year-old boy can't stop a killing. He just isn't strong enough. And he will probably be killed too.

Bill walks a short way up the street and calls Miss Beech on the number she gave him

He returns to his lonely vigil. Time goes slowly. He begins to nod.

There is an incoming call.

"Is that Bill Taylor?"

"Yes, Miss Beech."

"No. I am Officer Fiona Benson. Miss Beech asked me to help you. Where are you?"

Bill knows the street but has to look at the number on the door. "Fourteen."

"Thanks. I know the street. I've been there. Stay out of trouble. Do not put yourself in danger. I will be there in a few minutes."

It takes more than a few minutes.

Officer Benson rings Comms and asks for assistance for a possible domestic violence incident. She lives not far away but everything is taking so much time. Why is it when you are in a hurry everything happens slowly?

She hopes that Alison gets the memory stick to her station. Knowing her friend so well, she wouldn't put it past her friend to wait until the rain stops so she doesn't get wet.

Alison Beech gets soaked. Her waterproof coat isn't waterproof. It is not even showerproof. Her shoes are melting, her feet are numb with cold, and that is just getting to the car.

She drives to the police station where Officer Benson works. She drives around and around because she cannot find a parking space.

"Fiona said I had to buy Big Girls pants," she tells herself as she parks on a yellow line. "So here goes."

She has never ever parked on a yellow line. She expects to get a ticket and a fine. Her first ever.

So be it. There are times when rules must be broken for the greater cause.

She holds the memory stick in her hand as she rushes into the station.

"Good evening." The man at the counter speaks calmly.

"Please, this is urgent. Officer Benson is my friend and she asked me to deliver this memory stick."

"Ah, yes. She's not here. Please come back tomorrow," he replies.

"No, you don't understand. She wants you to take this memory stick and find out what's on it."

He glares at her. "I can't do that Miss. It would need to go to specialists, and if it is not yours, we can't touch it."

"But it is part of an investigation."

The sergeant's voice becomes sharp. "What investigation? I am not aware of any investigation. What authority do you have?"

"Well, PC Benson's. A pupil asked for help and I took the memory stick from her and promised I would give it to Officer Benson."

"She's not here. I told you to come back tomorrow."

Alison Beech raises herself to her full five feet one and says, "Sergeant, I am just the messenger. Please do not take a negative attitude. A police officer asked for my assistance in an urgent matter. She needs to know whether what is on this disk is evidence of a crime. If you will not take the stick, please find me someone who will."

The sergeant says, "I am the most senior officer here. If you have no official authorisation, I can do nothing. Goodnight, Miss."

Alison Beech walks out of the reception area back to her car. The car is as she left it. It has not been towed away and she has no infringement notice.

She does not speed. She does not drive wildly. She is calm and deliberate; nothing will stop her from achieving her mission.

"Bringing the memory stick here was a waste of time," she thinks. "I'll take it to the Central Station. This time I will stay until they take it seriously."

<h1 style="text-align:center">24.</h1>

It is still raining. The rain curtains the street lamps making everything gloomy. It is colder. Bill is sheltered from the drizzle as he sits in the front doorway of Lesley's house waiting for help; he feels the cold seeping into his bones. The blue denim jeans he is wearing are of no use in this sort of weather. The stamping of John Smith's feet as he crossed the room and the slamming of the door upstairs scared him. He does not live in a violent house and is unused to displays of uncontrolled temper.

Just as he feels as if he is a helpless child, two lights like glow worms appear through the sweep of the rain. They sway and wobble, sometimes apart and sometimes close. As they get near the glow worms cross each other, the higher one crossing behind the lower one then coming to the front.

The lights are on two bikes. Nancy Drew is on one and Hayden Millard is on the other. Nobody speaks. They wave. Bill leaves his space by the door and goes to them. They huddle so they can whisper.

"He got angry and stamped off," Bill whispers. He is shivering. Nancy takes off her wind breaker and puts it over his shoulders. She seems oblivious to the rain.

Bill continues. "I called Miss Beech. Officer Benson called me for the address. She is coming as soon as she can. Lesley is singing to let us know she is okay. When I called you, I thought he was going to get violent but it all seems calm now."

"Do you think you should tell Officer Benson not to come now?" Hayden asks.

They think about this for a moment. Without speaking they agree not to cancel the call for help.

"I'll knock on the door," says Nancy Drew. "Mister Smith can't complain about a girl, even a tall Black girl."

The boys would rather just leave matters alone and just stay on watch but they say nothing. They walk back to the front door. Bill stands on one side out of sight. Hayden stands on the other side. Nancy taps on the glass panel of the door. The singing stops. The door opens a crack.

"Hi Lesley. Are you alright?"

"Scared but okay."

John's voice is loud and angry.

"Who is that at the door?"

He is standing on the stairs, coming down. Nancy pushes the door open and enters the room.

"Good evening, Mister Smith. Sorry to call so late. My bike has a problem. I thought you might be able to fix it for me."

Hayden slips away from the door. He hurries to the bikes, now leaning against the fence, and slips the chain off the crank of Nancy's cycle.

John Smith explodes into anger.

"Was it you in the house with Lesley? Have you stolen my memory stick?"

Lesley begins to speak, "No Dad. What memory stick?"

He spins around and glares at Lesley.

"You! I trusted you." John is glaring at Lesley and waving his arms. "You brought your friend into the house, broke into my locked drawer and stole my USB. You thought you were smart but you dropped a picture on the floor."

Nancy stands beside Lesley as if to defend her. She thinks that Mister Smith will be angrier if he knows it was Bill with Lesley. "Sorry Mister Smith. The door hadn't shut properly. It opened when I pushed it. We didn't mean any harm."

"Liar!" shouts John Smith. He grabs both girls by their arms and pulls them towards the stairs.

"Take your hands off me!" yells Nancy, trying to hit him with her free arm. He takes no notice.

Hearing banging and shouting, the boys hammer on the door. John is shouting at the girls so loudly in a foreign language that he doesn't hear the boys. John drags the two girls up the stairs to Lesley's door.

"Go in your room! Stay there."

He pushes them and both girls fall on the bedroom floor. John slams the door behind them and locks it. He leaves the key in the lock so it can't be opened even if Lesley has a spare key.

There is silence. The boys stop knocking and listen. Everything seems quiet. They hear Mister Smith opening cupboards as if searching for something. Bill looks at Hayden and they both shrug. Lesley and Nancy Drew will shout if they need help. They return to their listening post.

Rose Knowles arrives. She has run all the way from her house. "What's going on?"

Bill says, "Shh. Just whisper. Mister Smith is really angry. He found a paper on the floor in his bedroom so he knows we opened his drawer. He knows we took his USB memory stick."

Hayden says, "Nancy went in and pretended she was with Lesley. He grabbed them both and took them upstairs. Now he's downstairs looking for something."

"Will he see us if we look through the glass?" Rose asks Bill.

"Yes. But you try, you're a girl. Tell him you are with Nancy and her bike is broken. You are worried she has been so long."

"Good thinking," says Hayden.

Rose knocks on the door.

"Who's there?" calls John Smith.

They hear his loud breathing as he walks towards the door. Although his voice is loud, he doesn't sound angry.

"Mister Smith, it's Rose Knowles. I'm with Nancy. Can you fix her bike?"

"You'd better come in," says Mister Smith. Although his voice is loud, he doesn't sound angry. Is playing a trick? The boys hear his loud breathing, as if he has been in a race, then the door opens.

Outside the door, Bill presses himself into the corner. Hayden is at the side of the opening. Even though he presses himself hard into his corner, he is still visible.

Mister Smith grabs Rose's arm and jerks her into the room. The door slams.

Rose is a small girl. John Smith hauls her on to his hip as if she is a wriggling toddler. He marches up the stairs, stands her on her feet beside him. He holds Rose's arm as he unlocks the door.

Nancy jumps at him. She is a big girl. Rose tries to hold his ankles to stop him from moving. Lesley joins Nancy as they struggle to pull him down.

He is far too strong. He flings Lesley to the floor. He kicks his legs and sends Rose sprawling. He pulls Nancy off and hits her hard on the chest. She goes down gasping for air.

The door closes. The lock clicks. John Smith leaves his key in the lock.

The fight didn't make much noise. The boys don't know what happened. They peer through the glass panes beside the door but a net curtain obscures details. All they can see is John Smith coming down the stairs and going into the kitchen.

Bill and Hayden stand nonplussed. They do not know what to do.

A smell of paraffin is in the air. From the kitchen they can see a yellow glow and flickering shadows on the wall.

They see John Smith leave by the back door. He runs along the path and down the street to where he left his car. Within seconds he disappears down the road. An oncoming car flashes its lights repeatedly as if to say, 'Slow Down'.

The oncoming car stops outside Lesley's house. Officer Benson gets out and stands by her car. There is a delay while she speaks on her phone. Then she sees the boys.

"Bill, Hayden. What is happening?"

"There's a fire, Miss," says Hayden. "Nancy Drew, Lesley and Rose are upstairs, we think. Mister Smith has just run away in his car."

The yellow glow has turned to orange. The smell is strong. She sees the orange glow, smells the smoke. For the second time she takes out her mobile phone.

"Come away boys," she yells as she waits for the call to be answered.

She calls out the address, then says "I need Emergency Fire Services: two ambulances with breathing apparatus, and police. I want the car I called in to be stopped and the driver held in custody. He is dangerous and may be charged with multiple attempted murders."

Bill and Hayden smash the narrow window beside the door. Bill reaches in with his arm but the lock is too far away.

Alan Pritchard runs up. He is dripping wet, his hair is plastered down on his head, and water is all over his face. He has run from his house but doesn't seem out of breath. He takes in the situation immediately.

"Officer, I can open it. Let me in."

Officer Benson and the two boys move aside.

"Don't look Miss," says Alan.

As soon as Officer Benson looks away, Alan goes to work on the lock. He has never seen it before but he has practised on similar locks. He seems to take forever but the lock is open within half a minute. In that time the fire has grown enormously.

Officer Benson can see an electric heater on the kitchen floor with the remains of a plastic paraffin bottle burning at the centre of the blaze. Lesley's bedroom is directly above. The ceiling is alight already.

"Wait. Do not follow me," she says as she races up the stairs.

The boys follow her. On the landing Bill says, "The room on the left."

"The door is locked," says Officer Benson. "There is no key."

John Smith has removed the key. Left in the lock, it would be evidence of murder. Alan steps forward. This is a lock he is very familiar with.

"Look away, Miss."

It takes him just five seconds. The group rushes into the room. Smoke is coming up through the floor, which is very hot. The carpet is smouldering in places.

There are no girls.

"The bathroom," says Bill.

He throws open the en suite door. The air in the room is thick with smoke and is too hot to breathe without choking.

Nancy is conscious, lying in the bath. Rose is unconscious on the floor. Lesley is in the shower on the floor. Her eyes are closed against the stinging smoke and she is coughing and choking alternately.

Alan says, "When you leave take a deep breath and hold it until you are out of the house."

Officer Benson has a mental chuckle hearing the advice she gave during a Civics lesson. She picks up Rose and hands her to Bill. Bill easily manages Rose's weight. He sucks in a deep breath because he knows there may be no oxygen outside this room. He hurries away to the stairs where he slows a little in case he trips. He holds his breath. He repeats to himself 'Keep going, don't breathe, keep going don't breathe'.

His lungs are bursting as he reaches the door and fresh air. He is safe and so is Rose. He sinks to the ground where helping hands take Rose away . A breathing mask is put over his mouth and nose.

Time is running out. Hayden grabs Nancy and pulls her up. Her eyes are wild and full of tears – later she says it was the smoke – and she holds on to Hayden as he helps her from the empty bath. She is too heavy for him. Her feet crash to the floor and her dragging heels slow Hayden down. He is holding his breath and already he is struggling. He knows if he breathes in the smoky hot air will choke him and he will die.

Alan grabs Nancy's feet and lifts. He is surprisingly strong. With Alan at the front holding up Nancy's lower half and Hayden at the back using his arms under Nancy's shoulders, the ungainly threesome makes its way across the smouldering floor. Nancy gets bumped as they go down the stairs with the tallest person in front.

Hayden makes it to the bottom of the stairs before his breath is absolutely exhausted. An old man wearing a Covid mask grabs his arm and helps him forward. The old man lifts Nancy from Hayden's arms. Without her weight he manages to make it to the door where two fire attendants in breathing suits are just entering. One grabs Hayden as he collapses. The other is a woman who takes Hayden's place. Alan's breath expires outside the house. He breathes fresh air and doesn't need the O-mask he is offered.

The old man hands over Nancy to helpers who rush forward. They try to restrain him but the old man turns back, trying to find Lesley. A fire officer grabs him. He fights with her but stops when he runs out of strength and falls to his knees. The fire officer places a mask over his Covid mask.

"Name?" she asks.

"Sam Bennet."

He accepts he can do no more. He puts his hands over his face, fingers upwards as he cries in frustration at not saving Lesley.

"Thank you for helping Mister Bennet. Please leave it to us now."

She escorts him outside where he is taken to an ambulance. The mask is replaced with an oxygen set. He is driven off to hospital. He will be in recovery for several weeks. A photograph of Sam Bennet appears in the morning paper. He is a hero for a second time. The first was long ago but nobody remembers it. He can't even remember where he put the medal.

There is still one rescue to make. Lesley. In front of the en suite the floor is burning with flames and smoke flaring up between the buckling boards like weeds growing on a tennis court. Officer Benson uses a fireman's lift that she has practised so many times in her job. She lifts the girl easily, sucks in a last breath and then follows the others out of the en suite, across the room and down the stairs.

She is fit, strong and trained for this situation. The air is so hot she feels her hair singe. She wants to run but knows that is dangerous; she could trip, fall, run out of breath, pull a muscle and collapse – before she finishes the list, she is outside.

The air feels freezing after the heat in the en suite and on the stairs. She can't remember going through the lounge. Willing hands grab for Lesley but Fiona Benson will not let her go. She can't see. She can only feel Lesley falling from her grasp. She struggles to hold the girl. She fights the hands and then falls to her knees.

"It's alright Officer," says and attendant. "You are safe now. Let the girl go so we can put a mask on her."

The calmness of the attendant does the trick. She releases Lesley and allows the attendant to treat her for smoke inhalation. Sirens and bells, whirling blue and red lights and spotlights and floodlights blind the rescued. Willing hands take the choking victims away for attention.

Fiona falls to the ground unnoticed in the surge of helpers trying to save any other victims. There are none. Lesley is the last.

Alison Beech arrives. She sees her friend needs help and calls a man over. Together they roll Fiona onto a rescue stretcher. Her clothing is stuck to her skin. Her hair has burned off across her forehead to halfway to her crown. She is semi-conscious, aware but unable to do anything. To help herself

25.

I know I am waking but I have a long climb to come out of my darkness to the light.

I hear a woman's voice. "PC Fiona Benson's photo is in the paper, and on television. She is a real a hero."

"Heroine?" I think as I wake up struggling to breathe freely. I know immediately that I am in hospital. I recall the choking smoke and intense heat of the fire. What evil force made Dad do it, kill me and my friends? I can't believe a man who has loved and cared for me all my life could do that. I feel vaguely that it was for our own good but nothing makes sense to me.

I remember Nancy Drew getting us into the en suite bathroom. Shutting the bathroom door saved our lives. She was awesome. And so was Rose. I must have blacked out for there is a patch I can't recall. I was in my mother's arms. I couldn't remember what she looks like. She looks young and she came to save me. She carried me like a baby in her arms through the smoke and the flames. Is she alive?

"You're awake at last," says the Indian nurse.

I have been awake too long. I cannot stay awake to listen to the nurse.

"I have to sleep now," I tell her as I close my eyes.

A different nurse wakes me for what she calls my Obs. She checks my blood pressure and how hard I can blow into a plastic thing with a blue ball in a tube.

"Blow hard," she says. "Wow! That is brilliant!"

The ball hardly moves. I hate it when people say you've done well when you haven't. After puffing I am short of breath and my chest is tight.

Some doctors come around. The senior doctor is a woman.

"Your hair will soon grow back," she says. "Don't worry, you'll be beautiful soon. I think you can go home in a few days."

Home?

Where is that? My house is burnt down. My Dad tried to kill me. He is in prison on remand but he will not be coming home. I have nobody and nowhere to go.

The nurse sees me crying.

"What's wrong, dear?"

"I have no house and no family. I am all alone."

"I don't think so. You have some very special friends."

Next thing, she wheels someone in. She backs into the room I am in, so at first, I can't see who it is.

Officer Benson. Fiona.

It was not Mum who rescued me, carried me through the flames and the thick black smoke. It was Fiona.

She risked her life for me. Her hair is burned off in front. She has no eyebrows. Her face is puffy and her eyes are so swollen they are just slits.

"How long have I been here?" I ask,

"Two days. Bill, Alan, Rose and Nancy are the same. Hayden is in a private clinic. We have all been kept sedated while we heal. My boss came to see me earlier today. They want to give me a medal. I said to give it to the kids."

"We were a bit silly thinking we could stop Dad. He was far too strong. What's happened to him?"

"He was arrested. In Denmark. He flew there in a private plane. He had three-year-old Sally with him. We are flying Sally's mother to Copenhagen to identify the child. She was out of her mind when Sally was stolen."

"I don't think he is my father," I say. "But I loved him to bits. He was such a good Dad. Do you think he stole me?"

"We think another man did the stealing, but your father is being charged with helping the other man. Your Dad's real name is Markus Vasiljefs."

"He told me that. "

"He is from Latvia. We think the other man is a member of the Dragon's Breath secret society. In Latvia they are called the Puka Elpa syndicate. They are trafficking Eastern European women and selling drugs and pornography. They have stolen children before. The memory stick has three different children on it. You are the last. But your father knew what was going on and for that he will go to prison."

I thought of the love Dad had given me, of how happy we were together. I say, "I miss him. I was so happy with him. He really was my Dad."

I feel the need to make excuses for him. "Perhaps I got lost, you know how little kids wander off, and maybe he found me and couldn't find my parents so he kept me."

Officer Benson doesn't comment immediately because she is a police officer and Dad broke the law by keeping me as surely as if he stole me.

"It sounds like he was a good father to you. He is not allowed back in your life because he tried to harm you. So, we might as well search for any relatives you may have. May I take your DNA and see if it matches any parents of stolen children?"

I have often thought of testing my DNA but not because of Dad. I had no reason to believe he was not my father. It just seemed cool to find out if I have Viking blood in me, and if not, where my red hair came from.

"When I am free to go home," she says, "would you like to come home with me and keep me company? I live on my own."

My heart is filled with joy. Staying with Officer Benson will give me time to sort my life out.

"Yes, please.

"Will you stay with me while we search? While we find your real family?"

"Yes. Not because I have nowhere else to go but because I really like you. I think you need a kid, one who is independent, maybe one who cooks a meal when you are working late. I need a home. I need my independence but I also need a mother. As Alan would say, it's a good deal both ways."

"You could call me Fiona, like a sister who's twenty years or so older than you."

"What about your work? Are police allowed children?" It is a stupid question. "I mean, with your shift work and everything."

Fiona laughs, a lovely tinkling laugh that makes me laugh too.

"I would be better off with a child to look after," she tells me. "At the moment I do far more hours than I'm paid for."

The hospital room seems brighter after she leaves. The sun manages to hit one corner and lights the whole room with a golden glow. The meds are wearing off. I have pain all over me. I want to scratch but if I do the skin will peel off and I will bleed. I have a light cotton top with deep arm holes that can be embarrassing if men or boys are around. My arms and my head took the bulk of the flames. They are kept bare so the air can heal them. They are crusting over nicely, although my arms look like the legs of a boiled lobster. I ring for more pain killers. They put me to sleep.

I become aware of someone sitting by my bedside. It is Miss Beech. I drag myself awake. I stretch and shafts of pain go through my arms.

"Hello, Miss Beech," I mumble. "What time is it?"

"Around five in the afternoon."

She looks too young to be a teacher. Her cheeks are puffy and she has shadows under her eyes. If she were older, they would be big black bags. She sits down on the chair next to the bed.

"You shouldn't cry," I say, trying to be kind. "You are too pretty to have bags under your eyes."

I meant to be kind, I really did; but she looks pole-axed.

"Does it show, Lesley?" she asks.

"Only a woman would see it," I tell her. "Sorry. The drugs make me say things that are rude. Well, not really rude like that, but quite nasty."

Miss Beech nods. She understands. "I've cried and cried because I let you all down. I'm meant to be the one looking after you. Instead, I ignored what you were saying. I nearly killed you by forgetting to give the USB stick to Officer Benson."

Suddenly I am the grown-up and Miss Beech is the child. Okay. No problem.

"It doesn't matter. It needed a technician to open it. Anyway, we may be kids but we can look after ourselves. You are kind and caring and we all love you."

I'm not sure if that last bit is right but at least some of us do.

"Really?"

Really which one? Kind and caring or love you?

"Hayden would have phoned Officer Benson. In any case, Mister Taylor would have called the police. And we all love you as a teacher because you are kind."

"Oh, yes. I suppose. Anyway, how are you?"

In pain, half out of my mind on painkilling drugs, stiff and sore, my skin shrieking from the burns. How do I feel?

"I feel fine. I'll be out of here in a few days."

"It's awful about your father. The police caught him. He's in Denmark," she tells me. "It's in all the papers and on every television screen."

"He is a good Dad," I protest. "He loved me and looked after me after I lost my real parents."

"Why did he try to kill you? Was it to make way for the new child?"

I am not sure why but I can often see past the obvious.

"That is the obvious answer but there is a chance he did not want the gang to torture me or use me as a sex object."

Wow! What corner of my mind did that come from?

She replies calmly. "I know in wartime some people kill their children for that sort of reason; like a mercy killing."

I am happy with that thought. It matches the love Dad has shown me all my life.

"I am glad you called Miss Benson," I say. "Dad got it wrong with the secret police. He also got it wrong with the gang. I think it was just one man who was exploiting Dad's fears."

"You're a deep thinker, Lesley. I visited Fiona Benson earlier. She told me she is going to be your mother. Can I be your Auntie Alison?"

"I would like that a lot," I tell her. "You will be a lovely Auntie."

"You are tired. Let me give you a kiss to say goodbye."

She kisses me on my forehead. The pain of it nearly makes me scream. I love it but the pain lasts long after Auntie Alison has gone.

26.

Alan and Bill are ready for release before me. They have been in a ward together. They come to visit me, one by one. Bill doesn't say much. He stands at the side of the bed, looking embarrassed and out of place.

"Boy, am I glad to see you," I twitter. "Bill, you are so brave and strong."

He lowers his head while he searches for words.

" You were too. And smart as well," he says.

"So smart I almost killed everyone," I reply. "How are Alan, Nancy Drew and Rose?"

"Like you, in an isolation room. I asked a nurse and she said they will be out in a couple of days."

He hesitates, then speaks all in a rush of words. "Look, your Dad is gone. Your house is gone. Why don't you come and stay with us? You can have your own room. Mum and Dad said to ask you."

"Oh Bill, that is so kind. But I think Welfare want to sort something out and I will wait for them."

I know. I am being tricky. Yes, Welfare is sorting things out, but they are sorting out things so I can live with Fiona.

Bill and I chat for a little longer, then he leaves.

Alan comes next. While Bill's brown skin hides a lot of the damage from the fire. Alan looks awful with blue bruises and bright red patches and brown scabs on white skin.

"You are an oil painting!" I laugh.

They don't stay long but it is so good to see them.

Hayden arrives. His dad brings him from a private clinic. Mister Millard sits on a chair against the wall. Hayden sits on the end of the bed. Every time he moves my body hurts like fury but I say nothing. I am just thrilled he is here.

"Alan has a problem. There is nobody to come and get him," Hayden says, "They asked him for his parents' phone so they can come and get him. He packed a sad and said he felt ill. But they will be back."

"I'll talk with Officer Benson, Hayden. I am sure she and Miss Beech will sort something out."

Hayden's dad says, "Sorry to interrupt. Nice to meet you, Lesley. I am cross with you for putting Hayden's life in danger."

"Mister Millard, Hayden was a brave young man who risked his life to save three girls. He and Alan carried one girl to safety. I expect Hayden will get a medal for being brave."

"Really? A medal? That would be grand. Well, we must be off."

His sour mood seems to have disappeared at the thought of fame. He pushes Hayden in front of him as they leave the room.

It is nice not to be in isolation, to have people come and go. I know the nurses are making sure people visit one at a time and don't stay long, but my visitors cheer me up no end.

A wheelchair squeaks into the room. Nancy is pushing Rose. Rose's head is covered by an elastic bandage. Her small face is black with scabs. Her eyes are still bright and she smiles.

"Can't speak," she croaks. I guess her throat has been burned.

"Will it get better?" I ask.

She nods.

You can't see the bruises on Nancy's dark brown skin – she's from Nigeria – but the pink of the scabs makes me laugh. Nancy Drew's head is burnt at one side. Some dark stubble like a man's beard has sprouted. I laugh.

"Okay, okay!" she laughs. "You want to look at yourself in a mirror, sister!"

I realise that there is no mirror here, not even in the bathroom. There is not much wrong with my legs so I will go for a walk and find a mirror and check on how I look.

"You don't want to look in a mirror yet," says Eloise, my nurse from the Caribbean as she swings into the ward. "I have to get you ready for your new home."

"With Fiona Benson?" I ask.

Rose and Nancy are shocked. Their mouths drop open.

" Officer Benson?" says Rose from her wheelchair.

"Yes!" I squeal. "She is my new foster mum!"

"No, Mister and Mrs Davidson," says Nurse Eloise. "Someone from Welfare is coming to take you in the next hour."

"No, that's not right," I protest.

But it was.

<h1 style="text-align:center">27.</h1>

I won't tell you much about the next few hours. I threw one of my famous tantrums. It did no good. I was washed (again) and dressed in brand new clothes: the top is quite good, a sort of flowerpot colour with a Happy Face on the front, a vest, and a small bra. I didn't wear the bra. Jeans are jeans but these are baggy, like boys wear. I hope I can change them when I get to my new home.

I am sent to wait near Reception. I am no longer twelve growing up; I am a child of twelve.

I don't have to wait long. That's just as well because I am getting into a furious mood. Two ladies come for me, Miss Manson and I don't know the name of the other. I have a quiet chuckle that it takes two officers, not one, to deal with me. I think they are the women from the silver car who have been spying on me. It if wasn't for them Dad would not have exploded.

I cross my fingers, close my eyes and wish bad things for them.

Actually, the home Miss Manson found for me is not too bad. It is a bike ride from school, or a twenty-minute walk, the same as my old home. There is a small garden. The house is a bungalow not a two-up one down like I am used to. There are two bedrooms. The smaller room is for me. I have had smaller bedrooms in the past so I am not bothered.

Paul and Mary Davidson are kindly churchgoing people. They have a cat and a dog but no children. They are in the early forties. The dog is a snappy little Jack Russell terrier. He doesn't like me and sulks in his bed by the back door.

Mitzi the cat has a loud purr. She loves sitting on my lap. Her fur is patches of brown and ginger on a white background. I miss poor old Rupert Rabbit. He got burned in the fire. I can talk to Mitzi instead but I don't know if Mum will hear me.

"We desperately wanted to have children," says Mary Davidson. Because of my age they tell me to call them by their first names. "It hasn't happened. I just have miscarriage after miscarriage. Now the doctor says it will never happen. But God has been kind and given us you to love."

I would rather he had given me to Fiona Benson. I am not religious but I am not going to argue with an omnipotent power. (That's my new world but I don't know if it is OMNI potent or om NIP otent).

Before I can go to school, I have to have therapy. Guess what? When I go to Outpatients, who should I meet but Nancy Drew. She is just leaving the doctor's room and passes me as I sit waiting.

"Hey, Snob!" I call. "Don't you know me any more?"

"Lesley! Crazy, Girl! Are you having therapy too?"

Dr Salmond steps out to meet me. She is a lady in her late twenties, like Miss Beech. She even looks a bit like Miss Beech but a little taller. She has a nice smile but unwavering eyes that see right into your brain.

We explain that we are part of a group caught in a fire, three girls, three boys and a police officer.

"I remember that," says Dr Salmond. "Why aren't you all coming to me?"

We couldn't answer that one; like why was I put with the lovely Davidsons instead of with Fiona. I like the Davidsons but I love Fiona.

Dr Salmond asks us both to come into her clinic. We talk about how my Dad tried to kill us so he wouldn't go to prison and how everyone helped keep watch on the house, and then the fire and Officer Benson and the boys saving us.

It takes over an hour but Dr Salmond seems not to mind.

"When do we start therapy?" I ask.

"You are having it already. Being able to talk about what shocked you is a really good start. You will have to go now. I can't make promises but to me it seems silly taking separate sessions with you when you all have the same problem."

And so, my healing began. Dr Salmond, "Call me Rosemary", organises group sessions plus separate sessions when they are needed. One day at therapy, in front of my friends but not Hayden, he has private therapy, Dr Salmond gives me a brown paper bag, a big one. I open the top and pull out RUPERT RABBIT!!!

He is scorched on his back and smells of the chemicals the fire people used to clean him. There is a note: "Found your cuddly, Lesley. He was in the toilet where you stuffed him for safekeeping. Love from the Fire Girls.

With Rupert beside me, I begin to sleep. I stop wetting the bed; I wasn't going to tell you that but it's true. After the fire I wet my bed. Every night. Partly fear of bed-wetting was what was causing me to not sleep. Enuresis is its medical name. You learn a lot when you have treatment. Encopresis is number twos. Thank goodness I don't have that!

Dr Salmond does even more. I don't know how she does it but Paul and Mary spoke to me one night about 'moving on'. Paul asks Mary to start.

"We know you are happy here," she says. "But we didn't know you already had a foster home. I have met the lady, Officer Benson. She loves you very much and rescued you from the burning building. Welfare turned Fiona Benson down because she is single and has night duty."

Paul takes over. "Last night we had a call from Doctor Salmond, suggesting we take another foster child, who was in the same fire and has been deserted by his mother. We can't take two children. You would have to go to Fiona Benson. We said it is up to you."

"It's Alan Pritchard!" I squeal. "Oh, please take him. He's a lovely kid. His step-mum abandoned him and his dad's in gaol. He has been living on his own for months."

"Yes," says Mary. "It is Alan. We've seen photos. He's quite a small boy."

Paul looks a bit grim. "We aren't meant to know stuff like that. Welfare said it's better not to know anything than can create a prejudice."

"He can't help what people have done to him," I tell him. "He ran into a burning building, forced open two doors and saved three girls; one was me."

I didn't mean to speak so sharply. "Sorry, that was rude."

"No," says Mary. "That was passion. What do you think, Lesley? You're a big girl now."

I tell them, "I love it here. I love you Mary and I love Paul. You are wonderful people. But it nearly broke my heart when I found I couldn't go to Fiona's house."

"We accept your view, Lesley," Paul says with a catch in his voice. "We would love it if we could be your aunt and uncle and look after you when Officer Benson can't."

I think he is close to tears. No matter what I do, someone is going to get hurt. "Having an aunt and uncle that I love would be super cool," I say. "And that would make Alan my foster cousin!"

It took a whole week but at last I am back with Fiona. Alan leaves the hostel and moves in with the Davidsons. Suddenly I have a mother, an uncle, two aunts and a cousin. I am never going to be alone again.

28.

It is not easy to go from living with the Davidsons to living with Fiona. The Davidsons had routines for doing things. Mrs Davidson volunteered her time at a charity that provided a lunchtime meal for those who couldn't afford to eat three times a day. She usually left the house at ten thirty and returned at two thirty every day except Sunday. On Sundays we went to church at ten and got home for Sunday dinner at twelve thirty. Before every meal we said Grace to give thanks to God for our food. We had evening prayers when television went off and before we went to bed.

Mrs Davidson's daily routine meant doing the housework before I left for school at eight. There was a different task each day. The work was less than I did when I lived with Dad because two of us did it.

After a week, the Davidsons bought me a bicycle so I could ride to my old school. It was very kind of them and meant I would heal more quickly. I left their bicycle for Alan when I went to Fiona's to live.

Finally, we are all allowed back at school. Hayden was to go a different school but he says he will ask his dad to bring him to Wootton School so we can all be together.

What a welcome we get! There is a special assembly. The six of us sit on the stage on chairs in front of the staff, looking straight at the pupils. Some kids pull faces and try to make us laugh. It doesn't work.

Officer Benson and Inspector Fry are guests of honour. He speaks about duty and women being as brave as men and how we all have to set an example for others and PC Benson did that brilliantly.

Officer Benson is asked to speak. She is in her fancy uniform; Dress Uniform she calls it. I polished the buttons.

"I want to address you all, and especially Years Seven and Eight. You are still children but like monarch butterflies, you are coming out of your chrysalises to become adults. Along the way you will get most things right and some things wrong. Learn from what you get wrong and others will celebrate you when you get things right. Like the six sitting here. They got it right. Adults wouldn't help them so they acted themselves when they thought Lesley was in danger. When things did get serious, they called the police. Good decision; you should always leave dangerous things to the people trained and paid to deal with them. I am proud to say these six took matters as far as they could and called for help when it was beyond them. We call that Courage and common-sense and for showing both, congratulations are in order. Inspector Fry?"

"For each of you, a medal awarded by the Police Department for Bravery in the face of danger. William Taylor, please step forward."

One by one we are given out medals. The newspapers have reporters and photographers. Three television channels are making recordings. These will be shown worldwide.

None of us wants to speak. It is overwhelming, scarier than the fire in some ways. After his turn, Hayden asks if he may say a few words.

"On behalf of our small group of friends. I would like to thank Inspector Fry for this award. I trust Officer Benson will receive something similar."

There is clapping for each of us, but after Hayden speaks there is thunderous applause.

Hayden raises his arm and chops down to stop the applause. "I wish to announce that I am leaving Kings Regent School and returning to Wootton High School."

There is loud cheering. Some staff stand and clap. Awesome.

I am last. Kind words are said by the Inspector, who hands me my medal. I ask for the microphone.

"I mustn't let Hayden have the last word," I joke. There is stamping of feet, laughter and applause. "Though I hate to admit Hayden is right, Wootton is the tops. Great teachers and wonderful friends prepared to risk everything to keep you safe. I came here after years of home schooling and part of a year in an awful school. I was so lonely. Now I have friends and support and awesome teachers, and one teacher in particular. Miss Beech. Education is not just about maths and English and science. It is about making sensible decisions. Without her Civics Elective we would be toast. Thank you."

The noise of the applause hurts my ears. It goes on and on. The teachers let it go on; they join in as well. Then it is over. The students leave row by row starting with Seniors at the back. It is time to get back to normal.

Now I am with Fiona life is different. Like me, she suffers from post-traumatic stress disorder. At night I hear her crying in her room. Sometimes I get into bed with her. She climbs into my bed when I cry or have a nightmare but it's a squash because my bed is small and I am big. Often, when she cannot sleep, she goes to the kitchen to make cocoa or drinking chocolate. If I am awake, I join her.

School is tough for a start. The Year Tens are the worst, always asking to see my scars, especially after my plastic surgery operations, which are almost constant. The Year Sevens are almost as bad. They want to chat about the fire. I tell them FBR: fire, bathroom, rescue.

Our group meets regularly for counselling. We also meet on Tuesdays and Thursdays in our Civics elective. Just as before, Officer Benson helps Miss Beech. I have no trouble with her name. Officer Benson sometimes uses our rescue in her lessons. We enjoy that because talking about what happened helps us heal.

I was so worried about Rose. There isn't much of her and she was the worst injured. She has made a good recovery but tires easily. Bill and I are close. Although his skin is brown, we are almost like a brother and sister. Considering how off-hand he was at the start he is very considerate now. He comes with me when I visit Uncle Paul and Aunt Mary Davidson. When we go there, we meet with Alan. He is a joy. He and I are both without parents, at least until his father leaves gaol. He is hoping the Davidsons can adopt him.

Nancy Drew is still Nancy Drew. She and Hayden are close friends. Hayden was scared his Dad would object to a friend who is a person of colour. Hayden told me it was difficult for a start but is good now. Hayden is the most changed. Now he is a hero and gets lots of attention he is kind and helpful. The girls rave over him but Nancy is his BFF. He has been asked to go on the Student Council to represent Year 8 students.

Life is good. The only cloud on the horizon is Dad's trial. Actually, there are two trials. The first starts on Monday and is about being in possession and selling material for the purpose of sexual arousal. What a mouthful for pornography! Fiona explained Dad's involvement was not hard core but is still a crime because his photographs show underage children. (Me)

The videos are another matter. Fiona says they were not about me but I am too young to see them or hear what they are about. I can guess.

This is a different charge with a prison sentence if he is found guilty. Alan laughs and says it's nice to have a friend who whose dad is in prison. I have to go to Court on Monday. If called I will be asked if Dad ever acted inappropriately to me.

The answer will be NO.

There won't be much sleep tonight.

29.

Autumn has turned to a bleak Winter. The days are shorter, the sun is weaker, when it does appear, and the days are darker. I keep thinking about Dad's trial. Today's Court case is about whether he made and sold pornography, and whether he exploited me as a child in his care. The second bit is really serious.

I didn't sleep much so I am tired and irritable. Fiona and I don't talk about it. She isn't allowed to because I am a key witness. We talk at breakfast about what is going to happen when we get to Court, something I have seen it so many times on television that I am not worried. I should have been. Going to Court is nerve wracking.

"Real life is quite different from television," Fiona tells me. "The scale of things is intimidating. The procedures are impersonal, like the tide coming in and you can't stop it. People say things but they have their view regardless of what you say."

We drive in silence to the Court. It is an imposing building. Four storeys high, it is made of concrete and huge sheets of vertical glass. The glass looks black and forbidding, the eyes of a spider waiting to pounce. The building could be an office block of a big company except it is not welcoming. It is quite forbidding.

A shiver goes down my back.

If I get something wrong, will I go to prison? If I tell a lie I will definitely go to prison. Do they have prisons for twelve-year old girls? If I make a mistake without meaning to lie, what will happen? If I said I made a mistake, it would still be untrue, and anyone could get off by saying, sorry I made a mistake. Miss Beech is teaching us things like that in Civics.

We go through a revolving door. It is a very tall door with four blades pushing us through. It would be easy to miss your exit and go round and round, and the people standing with us in our cheese segment look as worried as me. As I? Which is it?

We step out of the glass quarter circle and stand for a moment. At the far wall there is a reception area. Fiona takes my hand. I can tell she is nervous, too. She parks me by stopping us, squeezing my hand and leaving me three steps from the counter.

"Wait."

While she talks, I look around. There are framed pictures on the wall. Some are really beautiful. Like this one, I think, looking at a picture of a beautiful lady whose skirt is so short you can almost see her knickers.

"Come on, Dreamy," says Fiona. She grabs my hand and we are off. Fiona knows this world. She joins a small queue. I stand beside her. When it is our turn, she is given two passes.

Most people are walking past us as they head for the lifts. That's where we go, to the third floor. There are double wooden doors. A uniformed usher stands beside them. He checks our passes. Now we have to split up.

Fiona asks the usher to take me to the witness room. The usher leaves me in the witness room with, surprise, my teacher Miss Beech. Miss Beech has taken a day off to support me. I feel great about that because the whole Court thing really is intimidating. No wonder Dad doesn't want to go to prison; he must be worried sick because he believes all prisons are the same and, in his country, Latvia, they would find a way to kill him.

I don't know if that is true but he certainly believes it. Before the trial he got permission to meet with me. I sat with Fiona on one side of a sheet of glass. He sat between two guards on the other. He told me that he loved me and hoped I could forgive him. No way. He tried to kill me and my friends.

But this trial is about selling dirty pictures of naked girls. Girls like me. What if some sleaze comes on to me and says, 'Come on Darling. I know about you. I've got a picture of you on my bedroom wall.'

How embarrassing.

I know what is going on. Fiona recently showed me some of the photos he took of me when I was seven. The photos were innocently intimate like the embarrassing family photos everyone has of a child in the bath. That's all I'll say. Fiona won't let me see later ones. I can't forgive Dad for circulating these. I trusted him in my childish innocence. I feel betrayed.

But wait. Many of those photos are beautiful. I have seen a lot worse showing a lot more on cellphones at school. These photos he has taken could win competitions, I'm sure.

And that is basically what I say in Court. I am given a chair to sit on even though I am now as tall as many men. I am in my school uniform. I feel like I am in a play, on a stage with a spotlight on me.

I can sense the mood of the people in the jury. On the television you can see the expressions of actors but they don't show the raw emotions that I can see now. Curiosity? Calmness? Anger, perhaps?

I am quite calm. I speak to a microphone even though I don't need one.

"Please tell the jury about your childhood with Mister John Smith," says Dad's lawyer Mister Palmer. He is called a Counsel.

"Miss Smith?"

My mouth is dry. I give a little cough. My mouth doesn't work.

"Miss Smith, please take a sip of water," says Justice Montgomery.

I swallow a whole mouthful and splutter. Some of the jury giggle. I realise they are no longer angry. They are looking at me with sympathy in their expressions.

When I start speaking, my voice comes back to me from the loudspeakers. "I was very happy. I loved my Dad. He looked after me really well. He told me my mother and her parents were killed in a car crash and he was an orphan so I had no grandparents or aunts or uncles."

I slow down. I speak in phrases. I breathe in slowly during my pauses. What I hear doesn't sound like me. I sound like I am twenty, with a powerful voice.

I copy the Miss Beech talks to the class, looking at the pupils and holding eye contact. I do that to the jury. One older man in the back row leans over and fidgets with his leg. I pause mid-sentence and stare at him.

"Oh, sorry," he says, then focusses on me.

Still looking at him, I finish my sentence, then use my eyes again, sweeping slowly along the two lines of six people. "We moved house a lot, so I didn't have friends. Dad never touched me inappropriately and always knocked on my bedroom door or the en suite. I felt safe and happy."

I have more to say about Dad's pictures; that I should enter them in competitions, perhaps sell them on the internet now I have a smart phone. I tell the jury that I have seen sexier paintings in art galleries. I hadn't thought of saying that. I remind myself that if I exaggerate or say something I am only guessing, I could go to jail. That makes me stutter to a weak halt and my powerful voice through the sound system tells me I am now a squeaky-voiced twelve-year-old girl.

There is a loud silence. Is that right? Loud silence? You know what I mean. Then there is some clapping. The man in the back row stands up to clap.

The Clerk of the Court says, "Silence, please. There will be no applause in this Court."

Justice Montgomery says, "Thank you, Miss Smith. Mister Henry?"

Mister Henry is the police lawyer. "Miss Smith, at twelve you are an innocent child. Did someone write that very clever speech and ask you to memorise it?"

I know a put down when I see one. "No sir. At twelve I am quite able to speak for myself. Do you ask someone to write down your speeches and memorise them, sir?"

There are chuckles from the jury.

"Miss Smith, just answer yes or no please," says Justice Montgomery. She keeps a straight face but I can see she is holding back a chuckle.

"Are there any experiences where you felt more uncomfortable than would be normal in a family situation," asks Mister Henry.

"Yes." I wait. Justice Montgomery said answer yes or no. She finally gets it.

"Counsel, please phrase your questions for a yes or no answer, or clearly identify when you want a narrative answer. Even I could not follow what you wanted," she says with a wry smile. "Please answer this one fully, Miss Smith".

Point made. Can I trap this smart Alec who has got his mind made up already? I have to speak before he rephrases his question.

"No to the plural. Only one. I did have a recent experience with my father when I felt uncomfortable to the point where I sought a trusted adult's opinion."

I can almost hear Fiona give a sigh of thanks for not mentioning her name. She is sitting with the police team and Mister Henry. She avoids my gaze,

The Judge speaks to Mister Henry again. "Learned Counsel. Again, I find your grammar confusing. Miss Smith, you are correct. The answer to the Counsel's question is yes. But Mister Henry's intention by inference is that he wants you to tell the Court about any experience you had when you were abnormally uncomfortable. Now would you please tell the Court what that experience was?"

"Yes, Your Honour. Dad is a superb photographer. I saw pictures he has taken, especially those taken from his crane at work. I saw pictures of children when they were happy or sad or playful or withdrawn. I was happy with him taking pictures of me with no clothes on until I was ten years old. When I was eleven, I was not happy and did not pose as he wanted me to. At twelve I refused point-blank. Yes, I felt uncomfortable enough to say no."

Mister Henry has an ah-ha I've got you smile. He wants revenge. Will he fall for my trap?

"And what was the defendant's response?"

Time to spring the trap.

"He is a good Dad. He said we'll sort it out, and later asked if he could take shots of me in school uniform. I only had one problem with that."

Mister Henry fell for it.

"What was that?"

"He called me Poppet. I hate that."

There is laughter in the Court, so I wait before I continue.

"Dad is paranoid about secret police spying on people. He won't use a cellphone. That comes from his years in Latvia. To show he realises I am growing up and he trusts me, he gave me a smartphone for my birthday."

I have made my point. Dad is paranoid about secret police. It is on the Court record. I hope my paranoia comment can be used in his more serious case at the next trial. I want to help him but part of me hates him. Standing there giving evidence is making me think clearer than I have ever thought before. I begin to see what happened through his eyes.

I am taken back to the witness room where Miss Beech is waiting. At home she is Auntie Alison. She spends a lot of time with us. When Fiona is away for more than a night Auntie Alison sleeps over. She has given me awesome support in the months between Dad's arrest and this trial for trading porno material.

"Coming to watch?" Miss Beech asks.

"Sure, Auntie Alison."

We hold hands and the usher walks us back to the public area and places us in two empty seats.

"Well done, Miss," he mutters in my ear. "Cocky beggar but you took him down a peg or two."

The trial doesn't last much longer. This is the key question asked by Justice Montgomery, in her summary, before sending the jury off to make a decision. Here is what she said, as well as I can remember.

"Members of the Jury, Mister Smith freely admitted that he sells these pictures. That is not a crime if they are pieces of art created to give pleasure. If that is your undivided opinion, then he will be free to go home. You will recall the evidence given so clearly by Miss Lesley Smith that her father had a wide variety of photographs, including cranes, scenery, candid photographs of children and of herself as a young girl.

"On the other hand, to render a verdict of Guilty as Charged, you must be clear in your opinion that the pictures shown by the Crown Prosecutor's Office have been made essentially to arouse sexual feelings and are not primarily pieces of art."

The jury took less than an hour to agree that Dad was not guilty. He can't come home because he is on remand while waiting for his second trial, attempted murder, abduction, conspiring in a crime of human trafficking. That is me; he knew I was stolen but he kept me and told lies.

I am to be a key witness. I am really scared. At least there is no death penalty any more. I am conflicted; my head says he should be locked away for trying to kill us, my heart says I want to save him. I love him and always will.

As people leave the courtroom, our friendly usher returns.

"Miss Smith, well done all round. Justice Montgomery would like to see you in her chambers. This way please."

The judge has removed her robes of office, showing the neatly fitting navy-blue trouser suit she had on underneath. She is standing before a mirror while putting on lipstick. She is bigger than I thought. She is way taller than Miss Beech who is standing beside me, a little taller than me but shorter than Officer Benson, who is standing in a corner waiting for me.

"Miss Smith, may I call you Lesley?" Justice Montgomery asks.

I am uncertain how to address her. I remember the television drama, The Bill. My "Yes, Ma'am," seems to do the trick.

"Lesley, I take a very dim view of the circus act you performed in my Courtroom."

"I am sorry Ma'am. I don't know what got into me."

"I do. I have teenage children. That they would have done the same is no excuse for your wilful behaviour. I have cautioned Mister Henry that he must not treat child witnesses in that manner."

I feel awful. I can see myself not as clever but as a smart Alec, doing exactly what I was accusing Mister Henry of being.

"Having a high IQ does not make you clever, young lady. However, no harm was done but you must not repeat your actions in the next trial. A better Judge than I might strike your evidence from the record and that would harm your father, whom you obviously love very deeply."

I am not upset. I am not afraid. I am not weepy. Justice Montgomery is giving me good advice that should help Dad when I next give evidence.

"Lesley, I want you to know that your words helped the jury to reach their decision," she says. "They also help shape his future defence; a tormented life at a violent time of his country's history, and a paranoid state regarding personal safety where authorities are involved. Before his next trial, in which I will not be involved, he will receive psychiatric investigation."

Wow! She really listened to what I was saying.

Justice Montgomery speaks again. "I have spoken to your foster mother, Fiona Benson, who you see here in uniform. Please remember over the next few months that she has loyalties to both the Police Department and to you, her foster care daughter. It will help your father if you do not discuss matters with her. Miss Beech, you are deeply involved with Lesley's welfare. Could I ask you to be Lesley's sounding board in the matter of preparing for trial?"

What a good idea.

After we leave the Court, Auntie Alison and I go to McDonald's to celebrate. Rose the Nose has organised several kids to be there. It is a brilliant evening. Suddenly, I am very tired. Auntie Alison takes me home to Fiona's house.

As she leaves, she says, "Are you alright on your own, Poppet?"

My pillow hits the door as it closes behind her. I hear her laughing as she leaves the house.

30.

With school exams and sport and socialising with my friends and the lead up to the trial I have a busy life. I am happy when Rose is stronger. She needs long walks so our little gang take it in turns to take her out, usually in pairs in case Rose falls. Sometimes I am with Hayden, who can only do weekends, and sometimes with Nancy Drew. Alan lives with the Davidsons but sometimes he stays on after school and walks with whoever is available.

I realise I am never with Bill. That's odd. Nancy Drew is blunt and forceful when she needs to be so I ask her. "Nancy, why doesn't Bill join us on our walks? He goes out with Alan and with you a lot but not with me. What's going on?"

"Why don't you ask him yourself?" Nancy replies.

Rose the Nose knows.

"Lesley, you are both twelve," she says. "You have lots of time before finding a partner."

"I'm not looking for a partner," I tell her.

"You could have fooled me," says Rose.

I respect Nancy's opinion and I trust Rose. It's time for a chat. I catch Bill during Civics.

"Are we still friends?" I ask.

"Of course. It's just... things are getting much too serious."

No, they're not. I seldom see Bill these days. "Bill, I don't want us to get too serious and I don't want to lose you as a friend."

"My other friends tease me," he replies. "We are too close. It's embarrassing."

I am still annoyed with him.

"Will you help me with what to do with my Dad. Who cares what jealous people say? You and I have a strong friendship. That's all it is. We also have strong friendships with Nancy Drew, Rose, Alan and even Hayden."

I've got it. Hayden. I should have seen it earlier. He is jealous of Bill and is bullying him.

"Bill, I'll have a word with Hayden. Yes, I am friends with him but no more than anyone else. You are special but I certainly wouldn't marry you. Ever."

Bill seems to be chewing on something. He does that when he is thinking hard. "So, you need help with your Dad? The man who tried to kill me? Why should I help him?"

"Because he is my Dad, Bill. And I am beginning to think there might be another side to the story. Can you help me tease it out?"

Because there were two major cases against Dad. There is selling or making pornography and there are abduction and attempted murder so two different police departments were involved.

The first trial found Dad not guilty of having porn stuff in the house.

He has already pleaded guilty to abduction (read kidnap without any threats). He has yet to be tried for attempted murder. He will be sentenced when the trials are over.

The sentences get added together. If he has to serve fifteen years on each charge, I'll be forty-two before I see him again.

I don't think the others in our group could handle what we have to do, but I'm sure Bill can. Justice Montgomery said Fiona and I couldn't talk about Dad so it's Bill and me and Miss Beech. I will have to introduce her to Bill as my Auntie Alison. I don't know at the time how far reaching my decision to include Auntie Alison will be but I think she will be very helpful.

31.

I talk to Fiona about Bill and Dad. She is happy we are good friends who don't want to get too serious.

"We're only twelve," I tell her, "even though I feel quite grown up."

"What are you trying to tell me?" she asks with a smile.

"I want to take Bill with me to see Dad in prison."

"That's a big call. You know I can't go with you."

"Could I ask Auntie Alison?"

"That's a thought," she says. "I know you love him even though he tried to kill you. Why do you want to see him in prison?"

"He's my Dad, the only Dad I can remember. If you love someone, you forgive them," I tell her.

"My, you have grown up," she replies.

Miss Beech thinks it a tremendous adventure.

"I might even be able to take the Civics class there," she says.

Dad pleaded guilty to being an accomplice to abduction charges so he is kept in prison on remand until sentencing. I get one family visit a week, the same as a wife gets for someone on remand in custody, accompanied by an adult. It can't be Fiona. Name the day. Use it or lose it.

We arrange to go on the second Tuesday of each month in the late afternoon.

At first, Bill is quite discomfited when he calls Miss Beech Auntie Alison but he soon comes around because an auntie acts differently to a teacher. Bill confides in me that he is doing this for me; meeting his killer is going to be tough. His dad says no.

115

Auntie Alison talks to Bill's Mum on the phone. Next thing, Bill tells me his Dad thinks it will be healing. He will take his car and sit in the prison waiting room. That means he is worried but supportive.

The prison where Dad is on remand is a modern two storey building. It is made of concrete, painted white. It looks like a hospital but when you look around it is quite spooky. You don't have iron bars on hospital windows. The doors have locks on only one side. You go through a door, wait in a space, look at a camera and then go through another door that opens and closes automatically.

Although the room we are in could be the waiting room of any modern business, the uniformed guard sitting at a desk beside the only door makes me feel trapped. I imagine there is a torture chamber below us in the basement. I think of the horrible gadgets and machines I saw in history books. There is no view of anything but the guard at the desk. There are no windows. You can't see through the glass doors by the guard. They are like toilet windows. A buzzer goes bzzzzz.

The guard presses a button. The door swings open. Dad walks towards the table where I am sitting. A guard is close behind him. There are no handcuffs or chains.

I wonder what Dad is thinking. To see me in the middle of a white room with just the table where I sit and the black couch with Bill and Auntie Alison must seem weird. He is dressed in a tee shirt and jeans. The tee-shirt has a Mickey Mouse face on it. He has lost weight. His face is thin and a little haggard. The prison officer stands behind him after we all sit down.

Auntie Alison and Bill are on a black leather couch to the left, a small distance from me. I am at the table facing Dad. The prison officer is an older man, possibly a retired police officer by the look of his athletic body and the way he holds himself. He stands behind Dad. The man by the door presses a button and the door closes with a loud click.

"No touching," says the prison officer. "All hands on the table top."

I put my hands on the table and Dad does the same. We could touch fingers but we don't.

"I'm sorry Lesley," he says. "I just went crazy. The thought of you and the kids being tortured to punish me. I just blew up."

"Dad, I am well. I live with a foster mother who is a police officer. She carried me out of the fire. All of us were in hospital and still have ongoing treatment."

"I think your foster mother must be feeding you well," says Dad. "You've put on a lot of weight."

Dad, that's a message no young girl wants to hear! Don't you get it?

It is hard making conversation in a prison. My emotions are all over the place. I love Dad but I want to punish him for what he did. I am so disappointed in him. Strangely, I want to go back to us living together as father and daughter. Even though I have Fiona as a mum.

I must get on with why I came.

"Dad, I had no idea you were selling porn," I tell him. "How did that happen?"

"It was a time of war in the Crimea. In 2014 I was twenty. I fought against Putin's invasion by pretending to support the Russian underground while spying for Crimea. As Putin attacked, I was discovered by Putin's forces and taken to be tortured and killed," he said. "But a missile landed on the prison and I escaped."

"I managed to get to Lithuania where I was in a shelter for displaced people. It was an orphanage and as I was twenty, I was put in charge of younger boys. There was little food and soon the orphanage had to close."

So, he was not an orphan. What else was a lie?

"We were meant to go to a government hostel but us older men and women lived in a rundown building in a sleazy part of town. It was a jack up between a syndicate called Puka Elpa, Dragon's Breath, and the police. The gang used us to make and sell porn and paid the police to look the other way."

Ummm.

Seeing my puzzlement, Dad hurries on. "Some heavy gang leaders made me sell photographs. At first these were city landscapes and posed family photos. When I refused to sell pornography, they beat me up. Of course I had a knife. Everyone did. In the fight I wounded someone and he died. I had to flee to Tallin in Estonia. To cover my tracks, I took a job as a photographer in Riga, in Latvia."

Okay... I haven't heard of Tallin before but that makes sense. So does going to Riga.

"I learned to be a good photographer in Riga and worked there for quite a while. I made friends with Erich who had contacts with the Dragon's Breath gang and the Russians. He told me the Russian Secret Service had found me and were going to kill me that night. Erich had a consignment of drugs to deliver for the Dragon's Breath gang. We agreed to steal the drugs and sell them in Estonia. Eric and I used the money to escape on a ship. We ended up in Britain. There was still a lot of money left; we had been paid for the drugs in US dollars and diamonds."

Is he ghosting me?

"But Britain is different. You didn't need to sell porn here."

"Yes, I did. We couldn't touch the gang's money until it had been laundered. That meant selling the diamonds in small numbers. That took time. Until I got British nationality life was really hard. I worked on the cranes but the only jobs I could get paid slave wages. Under the counter, they call it. Then I was given residency and sent to a training school for crane drivers. I already knew my trade from Crimea so I came top of the class."

Dad smiles. He enjoys saying that he came top.

"The Dragon's Breath money was from drugs. I wouldn't use it. It is still in the bank. I sold my own photos until I married, and you arrived. Then I sold soft porn. But Eric said the gangs in England told me they would betray my new identity if I didn't sell hard stuff. I sold only a little to keep them quiet."

I love my Dad and I always will. He was there for me. He was never violent. But his stories do not ring true. I am twelve now and can tell when someone is lying. Dad has just given me the whole nine yards.

"Dad, I love you and always will. I will remember our time together with happiness. But I heard you tell Eric that you had to dispose of me and get another child. You stole a three-year-old girl and ran off to Denmark with her. Is that what you did to me? Was I riding a trike like little Sally? You locked us in a room and set fire to the house. For that you will go to prison for a very long time."

"And good riddance," called Bill from where he was sitting a little apart from Dad and me.

"Oh, Poppet. I love you. I didn't mean to hurt you and your friends. Rather than have you tortured and killed after suffering agonies, I believed it was better for me to be brave and kill you."

Auntie Alison is bursting with rage. I have never seen her so mad.

"Dad, this is the last time I will see you. The man I loved will stay in my mind but the monster who steals children and kills young kids so he won't be arrested is not the man I love. Goodbye Dad."

I stand and turn and walk away. Bill and Auntie Alison follow me. Nobody speaks.

32.

We are well into winter now. With all the talk of Global Warming, I expected a warmer winter but that is not how it turns out.

I have not seen Dad since the prison visit where I told him I was finished with him. I know I said that, but I really miss him. He was a good dad and deserved my loyalty. But he did try to kill me and my friends. I guess nobody goes to see him even though we have a visit a week to help him with his treatment for paranoia.

Auntie Alison comes to my bedroom and sits in the armchair. It is a pleasant bedroom. I have some posters on the wall, my laptop is hooked up to a large flat screen, my bookshelves are full. I have a woollen throw I can wrap around me if I am cold.

"Lesley," says Auntie Alison. She uses the couch when she sleeps over. It is a pull-out bed and quite comfortable. She is sleeping over tonight. "I am not hiding anything."

I am alarmed. When people say they are not hiding anything it usually means they are being sneaky. I wait, looking steadily at her eyes. She looks steadily back so there is no deceit.

"What are you not hiding, Auntie?"

"I want to take over your visits to John Smith."

Auntie Alison wants to see Dad?

"Why do you want to see Dad? I ask.

"Well, he is all on his own and you said you would never speak to him again."

"He tried to kill me," I splutter. "And two of my best friends."

"Yes, I know dear. I still have trouble with that."

"I don't mind, Auntie. I am starting to think he had a mad moment and was genuinely committing a mercy killing. In some ways, I would like to see him again, but Fiona can't take me."

"No, Lesley. I meant I want to see him. Alone. I want to read to him. He likes poetry. And he needs warm socks."

Warm socks? What is going on here?

"Auntie Alison, I'm fine with that. Dad is a lovely man with a lot of baggage. I would like to visit sometime, with you."

"Oh, that would be nice. I'm so pleased,"

We have snow for three days. At first it is exciting. School shuts down and Auntie Alison comes to stay to save heating two houses. Then the snow melts and we are back to our daily routine. The cold slush we walk through is unpleasant.

At dinnertime, the three of us sit at the table because we are having roast lamb. Auntie Alison has put candles on the table so we can turn the lights off. We are happy; warm and cosy, we have lovely food, and Christmas is just a week away.

The meal is over. We clear everything away and wash the dishes. Then we sit in front of the television. I lie back on the beanbag.

Auntie Alison is sitting on a recliner chair, with the feet thing up. "Lesley dear?"

"Yes, Auntie Alison?"

"John is having a heap of psychiatric tests and treatments and he needs some support."

"Support?" asks Fiona. She is in the other chair, with the foot thing down.

"I don't want to talk to you about it because the judge said not to," says Auntie Alison.

"It might be best if I write my notes in my room," says Fiona, a little crossly. "I've got a Court appearance that needs a lot of detail memorised so I can cope with the cross-examination."

The happy mood has gone. Although she is smiling, I can see Fiona is not happy with Alison.

"Lesley, can you contact the prison supervisor to ask for a weekly visit? John is having treatment for his paranoia and he needs to be grounded."

"What do you mean, grounded?"

"Well, he needs someone to talk things over with," she says. "To keep things as normal as possible. He is very much on his own. I know what that is like. You tend to go over and over stuff until you lose the plot."

I am not stupid. I know what is happening. Dad is working his charm on Auntie Alison. I feel betrayed.

"I'm not stupid, Auntie Alison. I think you are falling for him."

"I suppose I am," she says with a laugh. "Is it that obvious."

"Yes. And he is conning you the way he conned me. I've got something to do in my room," I tell her.

I flop on my bed. Boy! Is this a freaky situation. I am totally confused. I love my Dad but I also hate him. I love Auntie Alison even though she is my teacher. She wants to help him recover from his mental illness. She wants to see him each week.

I have often thought that Dad needs a wife to keep him stable. Isn't that what Auntie Alison is doing?

Should I be doing that, as his daughter?

But I'm not his daughter. He stole me from my family. My DNA test is not back yet but I am certain I will not have his genes.

I love him. He tried to kill me but if he really was off his rocker, shouldn't I help him?

I make a decision. I will make the visits weekly and I will go with Auntie Alison.

I tap on Fiona's door. I need to talk to her. She has papers all over her bed but she shuffles them together and puts them on the floor. We lie under the eiderdown while I talk to her.

Fiona is always sensible. "It would help if you went along," she says. "Sort of keep an eye on things. I think Alison is getting too close to this case. But you? Yes, I think you are old enough and mature enough to deal with the situation. Your boyfriend won't be so happy, though."

"Bill is not my boyfriend," I tell her.

"Whatever," she says. "Go and say yes to Alison and make sure it only happens if you are with her."

The first visit to Dad is awkward. Fiona tells me not to apologise or make excuses. John Smith has probably stolen me from my real parents and certainly tried to kill me. Dad obviously feels embarrassed.

"Hello, Dad." Same rules, hands on the table, no touching. Auntie Alison and I put our hands on the table and so does Dad.

"Hello, Lesley dear. Thank you for coming. I know you made a difficult decision to come here to see me."

Auntie Alison asks Dad what has been happening. He knows we will be coming weekly so has written a whole heap of notes on his treatment. I am happy to sit and listen. Eventually we leave. I have said just two words.

Over three visits, Dad and I start to talk. He tells me I can use his photos, enter them in competitions, sell them if I want to. He also gives me the PIN for his bank account. There are two. He tells me which one I will need to use his bank account.

"Lesley, please use the photos. They are not porn. There are many people who cannot have children. So, for them I invent a child. I cannot make babies, but I can take a child from about three and let the lonely people see her grow up. They pay me very well. Your pictures are helping fifty-three childless situations."

"Dad, what do you do when a girl like me grows up?"

"I take her on a holiday to Europe or Scandinavia and I disappear. The authorities look after her. I take a new identity."

"Do you ever kill her?'

"Absolutely not."

"Why did you start doing that?"

"I told you it was that or pornography. Half what I earn goes to the gang. That is Eric."

I have a flash insight.

"Dad, he's not really your friend. He is your guard to keep you loyal to the gang."

"I think you are right. Being in prison might be to my advantage. He can't manipulate me here. If he really is part of the gang, I would be dead by now."

I shudder.

"You need a new identity," says Auntie Alison.

"Not long to the trial," says Dad. "Thank you both for what you are doing."

I feel good. I think I am really helping him. I don't tell my friends what I am doing. I don't say much to Fiona either.

<h1 style="text-align:center">33.</h1>

It is time for Dad's main trial. The weather is bitterly cold. Fiona goes to work, leaving me with Auntie Alison. She has taken time off work to be with me. I am so lucky to have her. She is so calm and thoughtful. She is dressed quite smartly for today. She took me with her to buy a suitable outfit. I needed new clothes too, partly because I had grown even taller and have finally begun to fill out. I do not look anorexic any more, just skinny. I will be in civvies for the trial.

As it is winter and the days are quite dark, the Court House looks even grimmer than it did before. People are pushier and noisier. We are in a different court. It is much bigger. There are television cameras. I am asked if I want a screen when I am called to give evidence. I say no, remembering how I was able to communicate with the jury.

Then I find there is no jury. There are three judges instead. Only one is a man. We stand when we are told to, and sit when the judges are seated. Matters move more quickly than in the first trial. The Prosecution barrister is a woman. The defence barrister is our Mister Palmer, the man who defended Dad in the first trial.

The three judges give no clues; their expressions remain stony. They say nothing, leaving it all to the Clerk of the Court. Dad pleads not guilty on the grounds of temporary insanity. I think that sums up the situation accurately.

I am called early as a witness. This time I am in the ordinary witness box and no allowances are made for my age. There is no microphone. I have to nearly shout. Then I am cross-examined. This is straightforward, with no nasty surprises. I talk about Dad's paranoia and how I dealt with it. I am asked for examples and I talk about the Welfare lady and how Dad thought she was from the secret police.

The trial takes four days. I have to sit in the waiting room. I stay busy. I brought some school stuff along because I don't want to fall behind. I am allowed to use my phone but only in the waiting room. On the second day, I am allowed back into the Court with Auntie Alison. I did not know it until Auntie Alison told me that Miss Manson, the Welfare lady, would be in the witnesses' waiting room and I could not meet with her. Just saying hello would disqualify both of us.

It is a bit like watching a play. The Welfare lady is called to the witness box. Mister Palmer grills her about sitting outside our house. She tells him that is her job, to find children who are neglected, and take them away from their caregivers.

Then, surprise, they have not spoken until now, the judges question her. The younger woman, she looks a bit older than Fiona and is dyeing her hair red, asks, "Miss Manson, please explain to us why your job involves spying on people in their daily lives."

Miss Manson repeats it is her job.

Red Hair Judge asks, "Is that not spying on people? Is it not what is done in some totali..."(I can't remember the word but it kind of means Communist) countries?"

She means Russia, Latvia, Lithuania, perhaps even Poland. Dad's countries.

"No, Your Honour. I don't spy. I do my job," is Miss Manson's answer.

The judge says, "Mister Palmer?"

Mister Palmer half-stands and says, "Thank you, Your Honour. I believe you have found what might have triggered Mister Smith's mental meltdown."

I'm not sure what was happening next. The prosecution side got very agitated. Then Fiona was asked to speak by one of the male judges.

"Constable Fiona Benson, did you on that fateful night stop your patrol car outside number 14 Hazlemere Street?

"Yes, Your Honour."

"And was Miss Manson present at the scene?"

"Yes, Your Honour."

"Why did you speak to Miss Manson?"

Fiona said in a clear voice, "Miss Lesley Smith, who is now in my care as her foster mother, approached me while I was assisting with a Civics class in her school. She said her father appeared to her to be increasingly paranoid when a car from Welfare Contract Services was spying on her and her father, day and night. She clearly identified Miss Manson for me but was uncertain as to the other person who took over the surveillance."

"So, this was twenty-four-hour surveillance by more than one person?" Mister Palmer made his voice rise up as if he found the situation incredulous. "I find that is unbelievable and should not happen without due legal process. Constable Benson, did you later check that due process had been followed by Miss Manson?"

"No, sir. I checked before I spoke to Miss Manson. My call to the Communications Centre and the reply to the negative are both recorded and available as evidence to this Court."

Go Fiona!

"May I continue, Your Honours?"

All three judges are sitting upright. If they were dogs, you would think they had seen a cat to chase. They are on full alert.

"Please continue," says Red Hair Judge.

"I know Lesley, Miss Smith, from my attendance in her Civics class. I found her to be level headed and mature, as many twelve-year-olds are. I took her opinion seriously, that John Smith was showing paranoid tendencies such as locking them both in separate rooms at night, refusing to use a smart phone, becoming agitated when the school asked for family information. Knowing of John Smith's previous life as Markus Vasiljefs in Eastern Europe and Lesley's cries for help. I went immediately when her teacher Miss Alison Beech contacted me and said a pupil had called her to send help to Lesley's house as there appeared to be a confrontation and disturbance."

The male judge asks, "And this was on the night of the fire?"

"Yes, sir."

The mousy judge asks, "Constable Benson, you have implied that the combination of earlier suffering under a corrupt regime and a surveillance that should not happen in the UK without due process brought about a mental breakdown. Is that your considered opinion?"

"With respect Your Honour, I am not qualified to make that opinion."

I am right proud of Fiona. Although she is on the side trying to make Dad guilty, she has given him an out.

The three judges consider the case against Dad. He will go to prison for seven years for attempted murder, brought down from life imprisonment because of his love for me, his pleading guilty and his paranoia. He has to undergo further treatment for paranoia.

Auntie Alison releases an Exocet missile, "While John is on bail, he's coming home to stay with me."

"But you've only got one bedroom," I blurt out.

"That's right," she answers with a smile.

Embarrassing.

34.

But Dad never comes home. He is sent to prison for seven years. The sentences are concurrent, meaning if he behaves, they will be served at the same time. So, he is locked up for seven years, fourteen years if he misbehaves. My Dad won't do that. I don't know how it works but Auntie Alison got most of her bail money back. Fiona says Dad will probably be released on bail after five years.

Although we have our fights, Fiona and I live happily together. I still sleep over on Auntie Alison's pull-out sofa bed when Fiona is away from home. I can bring friends home for a sleep over. One night I had six friends stay the night. There were two boys, Bill and Alan and a new friend, George. They sleep in the sun room. The Rose and Nancy and a new friend Viv, sleep on the carpet in the lounge.

Dad did not steal Sally. I am so pleased. A man called Eric did. He was caught on a security camera walking with Sally while she rode her tricycle. He set up a plan that turned out similar to my case; he stole a child and asked Dad to bring her up. He employed a woman from another country to be a courier, to act as if it were her child.

Dad was coerced (have I spelled that correctly? Should I have said bullied?) into producing a virtual reality childhood for people who are childless. That's what the gang did to me, through Erich, who has an h in his name. Erich took away Dad's previous girl and gave him a new toddler, me. Erich admitted to stealing me at Heathrow Airport. Sadly, Interpol found the previous girl died of a drug overdose when she was seventeen. They are looking at her death as suspicious.

Dad is well now. Auntie Alison has been wonderful for him. Going to prison will bring closure to his old life and let him and Auntie Alison get on with their lives. I am to be a matron of something at their wedding. I will be eighteen or twenty then. That's a long way off.

I still feel rejected by my bio-parents. John Smith and I lived in plain sight. My Mum and Dad should have found me by now, which means they didn't want me, didn't care that I was lost to them.

I worry and sometimes cry in the night when I cuddle Rupert Rabbit. The faint scent of my mum has gone. I have lost my link to her. He smells a bit of smoke and disinfectant. Well, he did go through a fire and a toilet!

Isn't it funny how the worries you dwell on are often totally not so. I hate my bio-family for abandoning me. I have felt rejected all my life. Then you learn something and everything changes. That happens when I hear Mrs Walton's story. It makes me change my mind completely about my parents not caring.

Mrs Walton works for an adoption agency with a contract with Social Welfare. It is stupidly called Finders Keepers. Duhh. She replaced Miss Manson, who went to prison. Mrs Walton has been trying to match my DNA to a living person. She is an older woman, very determined but with fixed ideas, like a woman on her own cannot have a foster child.

We sit in the small lounge, Mrs Walton and Fiona in the armchairs. We only have two so I sit on a bean bag on the floor. I am still in silent sulk mood.

Mrs Walton says, "Your DNA is not from John Smith. As you suspect, he is not your father. He is no relation to you whatsoever."

Mrs Walton has more to say. "Your DNA is from a family named Lewis. They are English, not Latvian like John Smith. Your name has always been Lesley. Lesley Lewis."

So, my mother did choose my name. I want to keep it always, to remember the cuddles and the smell that gave me so much comfort. I have Rupert Rabbit with me at the moment but he is behind the chair in case Mrs Walton sees him. I reach out and touch him. Hello Mum.

"We found the grandparents first."

Grandparents? I thought they were all dead.

"Robert and Susan Lewis worked hard to earn the money to start a new life in a new country. A baby came along and slowed their savings. That was you. Three years later they were ready to change countries. Susan Lewis, her family name was Cross, is a teacher. Robert is an accountant."

I have grandparents called Cross. Wow! "Are they still alive, Mrs Walton? Robert Lewis's parents? . "

"Yes, Lesley. You also have two Cross grandparents. Both sets of grandparents know about you. They live in the south of England and are excited about meeting you. Both of your grandmothers cried when I told them you had been found, and I think the grandads had tears in their eyes too."

Suddenly I have four grandparents. I am so happy that my mother and her parents didn't die in a car crash and that my bio father's parents are still alive.

Mrs Walton gives me a moment before saying, "Susan found work in a school on the East Coast of New Zealand, in a town called Hastings. Susan's travel expenses, the airfares, hotels and baggage, would be paid for by the New Zealand Government."

"Mrs Walton, what about my father? Could he go to Hastings even if he didn't have a job?"

"Yes. The immigration agency said that as an accountant he should have no trouble getting work. But the payment for the airfares and the crates taking their possessions would only be paid in full if Robert was a dependent. That means he depended on Susan's wage."

I know what dependent means.

"The school year in New Zealand starts in late January. Susan's contract said she had to be there by the middle of January or she would forfeit travel expenses. They sold their house and furniture. With all their clothes and possessions packed, they said goodbye to their parents and caught the train to Heathrow. It was a very long day for a little girl who was not yet three years old. "

What? I was still two? I must have been big for my age.

"Heathrow is one of the busiest places on Earth. You got into a tantrum and ran away. The Lewises could not find you. The plane was ready. Their names were called over the PA. Robert stayed to look for you. Susan flew to New Zealand alone."

OMG. It was my fault! I threw a temper tantrum and ran off. I still do that.

I can't breathe. I am bright red. This is SO embarrassing. I am pinned on my cushion like those awful dead butterflies in museums.

Fiona tries to ease my feelings. She says, "Lesley, you were still two. You wouldn't realise the trouble you were causing. You must have been bone tired. Kids get grouchy when they are tired."

Mrs Walton continues. "Mister Lewis notified the police at the airport. People with young children were stopped and questioned. People leaving the airport to travel on by road were asked whether they had seen anything that might give a clue to your whereabouts. People going to the city by train were also questioned. Nobody had seen anything untoward.

"The newspapers and broadcasting media publicised that a girl was missing. They named her and showed the photograph Robert thought was the best likeness."

"It was before my time," says Fiona, "but I did study the case in my training. It was considered to be an excellent police response."

"But they didn't find you," Mrs Walton comments. "Robert Lewis stayed in London for a month. It took him that long to get another flight. When the police received no more calls and every avenue had been explored, he joined his wife in Auckland."

"Lesley is not that common a name," I offer. "Didn't they check on that name? Nursery schools, play groups…"

"I'll find out for you," says Fiona. "But I think Mister Lewis will know."

She looks meaningfully at Mrs Walton, who replies, "Would you like to speak to your mother and father? I arranged a Zoom call for eight o'clock our evening time and eight o'clock in the morning their time."

She arranged a meeting with my parents without consulting me?

That is outrageous. I suck in a deep breath. My eyes fire lasers with rage. They are my parents and I am me. She talked to them but not to me. I'm leaving.

Fiona feels me getting ready to go. She puts her hand on my shoulder. "Relax dear, this is the way agencies always do it. Someone has to be asked first and that means someone is asked second. The main person is only talked to when any problems have been sorted out."

"Oh, Lesley! I am so sorry," wails Mrs Walton. "I should have asked you first because you are the youngest. I am so sorry, my dear."

She doesn't sound sorry. I am not her 'dear.' I am Lesley, with feelings. Those feelings are of rejection.

Mrs Walton you just don't get it.

"Mrs Walton," says Fiona in a calm voice. "Lesley has felt rejected all of her life. As a pre-teen she feels part adult and part child. I am sorry to say that you have not helped her feel like an adult with an equal share in this exchange."

Good for you, Fiona. You nailed it. That's exactly how I feel.

The computer lights up. Will we join the meeting?

I take control. That's what Fiona is telling me to do. She doesn't have to say the words. We think for each other now. "Would both of you please leave. I will take the call myself."

I think if Mrs Walton hadn't left the armchair by herself, Fiona would have pulled her out. There was another quick exchange of looks between Fiona and me. Complete understanding. I am to put my adult self to the task while Fiona can sort out Mrs Bossyboots in the kitchen.

This is a huge moment. My hand pauses on the mouse. I click.

A man's face appears. It is a nice face, handsome, maybe. He has dark hair and brown eyes that seem wet and liquid. His brow is high. His cheek bones are just right, like mine. Of course they are like mine. His voice quavers a little but is pleasant.

"Are you, our Lesley?

"Yes. The DNA says you must be my father, but I can't remember you at all."

"I want to talk to you one on one for a start," he says. "Please call me Robert. Have you had a happy life?"

"Yes." I can't call him Robert yet. "I had a lovely life with a man called John Smith. He told me my mother had been killed with her parents in a car crash and he was an orphan himself."

"I wanted to talk to you first because the lady in the adoption agency who found us says he tried to kill you."

I was to learn that New Zealand people use statements to ask questions. He is asking if I had been interfered with.

"He never hurt me or touched me inappropriately if that's what you are asking. I have been told he was originally a resistance fighter in the Crimea. He escaped to Estonia, then Lithuania and Latvia and later moved to the UK. He thought if he went to prison for selling what Fiona calls provocative pictures, he would be killed by either the Russians or the drug cartel in Latvia. Because of his fear of prison, he went off the rails. To save us from torture he burned the house down with me and my friends in a locked room."

"Oh. My Goodness. You are not kidding, are you."

"No. I still love him but he can never see me on my own again."

"I will explain this to Susan. What about now?"

"I am in a very happy foster home. Fiona is a lovely foster mum."

"But the lady at Social Welfare tells us the woman is on her own. There is no man. And she works full-time and often at night."

I suppose I should be angry but his concern is genuine. If this man thinks I am in a bad place he will walk across the oceans to protect me. My heart swells with his obvious love.

"I like Mrs Walton, the Welfare lady. But she has old fashioned ideas and her way is the only way. I didn't like the lady before her, Miss Manson, but she got fired for causing Dad's breakdown. She blocked Officer Benson from taking me at first. Officer Benson appealed and won. I am thirteen now and can legally be left on my own all night. With John Smith I was often on my own. I cooked and cleaned and paid the bills. I am quite competent."

Robert does not interrupt. He hears me out until I finish. Then he says, "Lesley, we are your biological parents. When we lost you, Susan had a breakdown. Losing you broke my heart. But we have moved on, as you would expect. We have three children, all boys. Susan is now a deputy principal in Hastings, a lovely sunny place, good for a holiday. "

I understand what he is saying in his Kiwi way. They have moved on; I have moved on. Let's get together on a holiday.

My whole attitude has changed from hate to love. In just a brief conversation. My bio-Dad is a great guy, full of love for me. I don't want to hurt him; I don't want to hurt Fiona. One part of me wishes I had refused that DNA test.

"I'll let you talk to Susan."

He carries his laptop through to another room. I can hear boys being boys in another room.

"Hello Lesley. I am Susan. I gave birth to you nearly thirteen years ago and then I lost you."

I take the lead. "Susan, may I call you Susan? I have no memory of you or Robert. I am sorry but you need the truth. To you, I was dead. Stolen and killed by some pervert."

"That is exactly right, Lesley. Spot on."

"I still have Rupert Rabbit. Do you remember him?"

"Oh, Lesley! Of course, I remember Rupert Rabbit."

"He smelt like you, so you were always with me to talk to. Now he smells of smoke and disinfectant."

With the thought of Robert Rabbit being my link to her, Susan begins to sob. She manages to rein in her emotions and says, "Sorry. I mustn't cry. It has been so awful, losing a child. Yes, we have thought of you as dead for some years now. That was clever of you to talk to Rupert Rabbit. Although I'm close to tears, I am thrilled you are still alive. And well cared for. I just want to hug you and hold you and never let you go."

This is awkward. Robert returns with three boys in tow. "Lesley, these are your brothers. They are little ratbags but in some ways they are cute."

"I am Liam," says the oldest boy. "I am eight. This is Gerard. He is six. George is only four."

"Hello boys," I manage to say. "I am your sister Lesley. I am thirteen. I had to stay behind when Mum and Dad flew to New Zealand."

I see Gerard using his fingers to squeeze hard and giving George a horse bite on his arm muscle. I tell him, "Gerard, don't bully George. I don't like bullies."

"Sorry Lesley," he says shamefacedly.

"Well done, Lesley," says my bio-Mum. "That is exactly what big sisters do."

Fiona comes through the door. She raises her eyebrows. I give her a thumbs up. I make a big decision. "Mum and Dad, I would like you to meet my foster Mum, Fiona Benson."

Fiona sits with me. "So nice to meet you," she says. "Has Lesley told you they have caught the man who stole your three-year-old?"

"No. When was that?"

"Some weeks after John Smith's trial. He denied any part of stealing children. John is a photographer, first rate. "

"He's teaching me how," I say.

"Shhh! They need to know your loss was not their fault. Don't interrupt," says Fiona to me in her teacher's voice. Then she talks to the screen again. "A man called Erich Schlieman is part of a gang of criminals in Riga. Erich stole Lesley and told John Smith her parents had been killed in a car crash and the grandparents died in a house fire. John was an orphan so there were no living relatives."

"Can you visit us in Hastings?" asks Susan.

"Are you coming to England, then?" Fiona replies.

"Sorry, Hastings New Zealand."

"I have been thinking of taking some leave I am owed. They are giving me a medal and a month's paid leave," says Fiona.

That's the first I've heard of a medal. I thought Fiona had said no.

"I'll chat with Lesley and her counsellor in case it could be very disruptive "

"I'm overcome," says Susan. "I think I will stop now. Can we arrange a weekly Zoom call?"

We don't always connect immediately with people but when we do, bridges are built as we learn more and more about each other. After our first call, I felt I knew my mother. I am taken back to when I was not quite three. I want her to hug me.

But this is now. I love Fiona but she is not my mother. I am torn between my biological parents and my foster mother.

Am I holding Fiona back? She is getting quite old and if she wants babies she should hurry up and get on with it. But how can she have a husband if I am still around? And I love my friends, and Wootton School. And Auntie Alison. New Zealand sounds exciting. Mum and Dad love me.

What should I do?

35.

It is still Spring but already the days are stinking hot. The local swimming pool is crowded. The water is warm which sounds marvellous but you can't swim for people.

Now I have been living with Fiona for five months, the flat seems very small. We are both big, so the flat feels small and cramped. I don't like the building. It is filled with single people, mainly. men.

Fiona is having a cool bath. When you fill the bath or use the shower, the water makes a loud roaring sound. When you flush, the lavatory sounds like Niagara Falls.

Fiona's phone rings.

"Fiona's phone, Lesley speaking."

"It's Brian Batchelor here, Fiona's partner."

What?

So, he is the male smell on her clothes when I do the washing.

"I'd love to meet you, Brian," I say. "Where can the three of us meet for a meal?"

I want McDonald's but that is not the kind of place Brian means. I tell him, "The Sorrento Restaurant. It's Fiona's birthday next week. I'll pay. I'll arrange the meal. You arrange the cake. Not too much sugar and definitely no chocolate. Seven o'clock okay for you? Can you deal with that?"

He sounds nice guy; prepared to let a twelve-year-old make reservations but checking he is not asking too much.

"I sure can."

I have money of my own, over a thousand pounds because Dad told me to empty his account and set up my own. Auntie Alison went with me to the bank. She is my guarantor. I invited her to the dinner.

Fiona thinks she and I are going for a birthday treat. Imagine her surprise when we are shown to a table where Brian and Alison are already reading the menu!

"You sneaky little sh**," she says to Alison.

"Lesley," Auntie Alison says, "Tell Fiona who is to blame."

"I'm not marrying you if you abuse your children," laughs Brian.

It's the first I have heard about marriage. I look at Aunt Alison's face. It's news to her too.

I look at Fiona's face. It is bright red and she is speechless. Brian gives her a kiss. Whoops. I think she was telling porkies when she said she had another overnight shift.

I like Brian. He is not as tall as Fiona; he is probably a little younger than her. He looks like a secondary school teacher. I am right, he is. And I am right about his age, twenty-nine.

So, what's wrong with him? Why isn't he married? He's good-looking, clever, polite and good with kids like me.

Alison does the job for me. "So, Brian, why do you deserve our lovely friend's hand?"

He lobs her service back at her. "I don't," he says. "She's too good for me."

Good answer.

"My first marriage ended disastrously. I am only slowly recovering."

Alison gives him a forehand shot. "So is Fiona."

Fiona says to me, "Lesley, come to the rest room, please."

The rest room is empty. We each sit on a toilet with the doors open.

"I am so sorry, Lesley. I have been meaning to talk to you. I wanted you to meet Brian first, get to know him, give your approval. Then my foster-daughter and I could plan the next step, marriage. After that, we could leave this flat and go to live in Brian's house like a normal family."

I hear her sniffle. I leave my cubicle and slip into hers to give her a cuddle.

"If you don't marry him, I will."

Fiona laughs her lovely tinkling laugh, but this one ends with a snort.

"Lesley, you can always manage to surprise me. You have made me so happy. Let's make this birthday really special; I'll ask him to marry me."

And that is exactly what she does. Alison and Brian are talking but stop as we approach the table. We sit.

Fiona looks at Brian. "Brian Batchelor, we are both emotional junk heaps who belong together."

Good move, Fiona.

"Apart from my Mum and Dad who are in Portugal and my sister in Canada, my three most important people are with us for my birthday, you. Alison and Lesley. In front of Lesley and Alison, will you marry me?"

I hold my breath.

"If you can put up with me, yes."

They are sitting side by side; Brian stands and puts his hands under Fiona's elbows and she stands too. Then, holding hands, he asks, "Fiona, I love you. Will you marry me?"

She says "Yes, my love."

We had forgotten where we are, in a restaurant with people all around us. People begin to clap, then someone starts to sing For they are Jolly Good Fellows, and everyone claps. An ice bucket with champagne appears.

I hope I am not paying for that.

The meals are free. Photos are taken. Time has flown by chatting with people, and eating and drinking - I only get Sprite. Then it is all over.

We have forgotten the birthday.

I start singing, "Happy Birthday to you… "

Everyone joins in. There is cheering and much clapping of backs. It is a wonderful time.

We move into Brian's house. He had to buy out his ex-wife Faye's share. I think Fiona helped with money. She rented the flat so it was easy to leave.

Behind Brian's house are a lawn and two blossom trees. It is Spring and it is as hot as Summer so they have finished flowering. They have lovely coloured leaves. One is a cherry tree. Brian says it has lovely sweet fruit. The other is an apple tree. Brian has a battery powered electric mower. It is my job to cut the lawns each week or when they look scruffy.

It is a happy time but it didn't last.

One day Fiona comes home distressed; Brian comes home tired.

I am tired, too but I make a pot of tea. It is Fiona's turn to cook dinner. I know she is too tired. At times like this, especially at that time of the month, I usually offer to cook.

"Lesley, do you think you could get dinner tonight?"

Hmmm. There are now three of us. Surely Fiona's fiance will offer to cook? I stay quiet.

"No. We'll get Chinese," says Brian.

There is a tense silence.

"I don't mind," I tell them. I get up and move to where some wiener schnitzel is thawing.

Wrong move, Lesley.

"Sit down, Lesley. I said I would get Chinese. It's time you learned to obey orders."

Brian's voice is harsh and bullying. I use my laser eyes and bore into his. He reflects my lasers and adds his own.

His way or the highway.

Fiona and I can still communicate without saying much. She wants me to obey Brian.

Brian huffs and puffs as if he is climbing Mount Everest. It is warm but he hunts for and puts on his parka as if going out into a blizzard.

This is going to end in tears.

<h1 style="text-align:center">36.</h1>

As soon as Brian leaves Fiona says, "Lesley, I need to tell you something bad. Erich has been wounded inside the prison and might die. A guard was nearby and tapered the assassin. He is Russian. John Smith will be moved to an unnamed prison,"

"Dad said that would happen,"

"He is getting a new identity. He is terrified that when he can't be found, the Russians or the gangs will punish him by killing his family. You."

"That's a clever trick. Most men would not take a new identity. They would just try to disappear."

"He wouldn't have a bar of it. I told him you were going to New Zealand to be with your real family. That persuaded him. He said he would take a new identity and serve out his time in another prison, maybe in Ireland."

"Is he safe at the moment?"

"Yes. He is in isolation. That's normally a punishment, and prisoners are often transferred to another prison. He will simply disappear."

"That makes my decision easy," I say. "I would like to go to Hastings. And you and Brian don't need a twelve-year-old kid while you sort out your relationship."

She gives her lovely tinkling laugh. I love it.

There is no more talk of her coming to New Zealand with me.

There are things to do. My passport is for Lesley Lewis, female. I cannot change either of those descriptions. But I can change my looks.

I have my hair cut like a boy's. I die it brown. It goes a lovely rich chestnut colour. Fiona buys me some boyish clothes; they are all the fashion now. I have a school shirt and school shorts like Hastings High; Fiona emailed Susan and got the pattern and a brochure.

I am worried about standing out. I am tall. As a girl I stand out. I don't have a bust and I am wide in the shoulders and small in the hips so as a boy (ugh) I won't stand out as much. My name could be either sex. Sorry, gender. Toilets might be a problem.

We cannot get flights to New Zealand straight away. Fiona finds a flight to Singapore in three weeks' time.

"My credit card is full," she says. "Well, not full but I don't have enough credit to pay for a return ticket."

"Make it one way, Fiona. I'll pay. I have enough money to get back to the UK."

If I come back.

That depends on Brian's attitude towards me. He is fine with Fiona; they are deeply in love. It's just me. He's a control freak and I just irritate him.

I ask Rose Knowles, Rose the Nose, about Brian Batchelor. Her uncle runs a detective agency. Snooping runs in the family.

37.

Bill Taylor comes to see me off. He is not as awkward with me now and shakes my hand and puts his arm round my shoulders.

"Goodbye, Lesley," he says. "If you are not home in six years I'll come and find you."

Romantic.

I kiss him on the cheek.

Auntie Alice and Fiona drive me to Heathrow airport. We have tea and cakes while we wait to be called.

"Let us know what you decide," says Auntie Alice, speaking for Fiona. I am not fooled by their matter-of-fact tone. I am also very worried about Brian Batchelor, who stayed at home and just said, "I hope you find your family safe and sound."

Hastings is on the east coast of the North Island of New Zealand, te waka te Maui, the canoe of the discoverer, Maui. I like the Maori name. The jet arrives early in the morning.

It has been a long and weary flight, with some downtime in Los Angeles, where my seat neighbours get off. Nobody comes to replace them, so I stretch out across three seats. Nobody seems to mind.

I sleep for a while, then I wake in panic. What have I done?

I have a perfectly good home, lots of friends, success at school, what more can a girl want?

A nicer Brian. As usual, I have left in a huff and avoided the problem. What a coward.

But Fiona needs to bond with Brian. They love each other. I irritate Brian. I am too adult and too bossy but as I am twelve, I need to be soppy at times and to be petulant and cuddle-yearning. I need to feel love.

So, give them some space.

Will I find love here in New Zealand? And if I do, will I break Fiona's heart by staying? Only time will tell. Sometimes you have to wait for an answer to show itself.

I get a taxi to the bus station. I have three hours to fill before my bus leaves for Hastings. I have one suitcase weighing forty pounds, a backpack and a computer bag. Although I slept on the plane, I am still tired.

I put my stuff beside me, my legs on the case which is flat on the floor. I loop the straps of my backpack and my computer bag around my ankle. I fall asleep.

I don't know how long I am asleep. I am woken up by a sharp tug on my ankle. My mind catches up. I open my eyes. Someone is stealing my gear.

I scream as loud as I can.

"Shh. " says a boy's voice. "I am Terry."

He stops tugging at the straps around my ankle. I look at him. He is brown, with long hair like a girl. . Although his hair is black, he has tinted the last three inches bright red and it is fuzzy and fluffed up.

He is wearing jeans and a bright top that he has knotted at the waist, He has a bright smile and a huge grin that shows his strong white teeth.

He offers me a bottle of Coke. It is half-full. He wipes the top with his hand and with a cheeky grin, says, "Here, take a drink."

I take the bottle, wipe the top with my hand and drink. I am so thirsty. When I stop drinking, I see I have almost emptied the bottle.

"Sorry, I've almost finished it."

"No problem. I didn't want it all. It's too gassy."

At that moment I erupt a gigantic burp.

"See," he says. "Gassy. What's your name?"

He seems honest but quite cheeky. Is he a junior con-man? Should I give him information about me?

"Lesley. Lesley Lewis."

He seems to know my name.

"Terry Te Tau. Kids call me terry tea towel."

"You're brown."

"Don't worry, it won't come off."

"Not even when you wash?"

"Not even then. I was behind you when you asked about the bus to Hastings. That's where I'm going. I woke you so you won't miss the bus."

Bus? I thought I was going by coach.

I look at my cellphone to check the time.

"We've got ten minutes."

"No worries. But let's get moving. I need your name and fifty bucks."

I don't know bucks so I guess and give him fifty dollars.

"I'm Lesley Lewis," I tell him. I show him the label on my case.

Terry Teatowel disappears. When he comes back, he has two pieces of paper.

"Our tickets," he says. "And five bucks change. I said you were only twelve so you get a discount.

A queue of people is lined up beside the bus. One man arrives after us. He has his piece of paper in his hand. He is wearing a hat that could be straight off any street in central London. He is also in a pinstripe suit. Perhaps like me he has newly arrived.

There are bags and suitcases in a jumble by the back of the bus.

"Put your stuff on the footpath," Terry advises. "Let's get on."

There are no seat numbers on my ticket. Terry takes a window seat. I slip in beside him.

"Isn't there a coach?" I ask.

"This is a coach. We call it a bus."

I can't believe it. "It's four hundred and twenty kilometres to Hastings. Buses run in towns. They aren't suitable for long distances."

"That's for real."

Then Terry is quiet. He seems quite shy.

"Are you the new girl? " he asks. "Mrs Lewis's missing daughter?"

"Yes."

"Hey girl, you're famous. Everyone knows about you. You were almost toast."

Oh, no. How embarrassing.

I don't reply. The bus is not comfortable. I must have chosen a cheap bus instead of a comfortable coach. I will be on the bus for over seven hours. It is noisy. There are so many bends in the road. You can smell diesel fumes.

Terry falls asleep. I close my eyes but I can't sleep. The bus is roaring and lurching and bouncing up and down. Surely this is not the normal way to get to Hastings?

After an hour my bottom is aching. The bus is vibrating too much to read my Kindle. It is hard to use my i-Pad. I put it down in frustration. Terry wakes immediately and grabs it. He seems able to read and write without any trouble. I guess he is used to buses.

We stop after two hours. People pile off the bus. Mister Suit stays on the bus. Terry is asleep again. I have to find a lavatory.

I find the lavatory behind a door at the side of the cafe called a milk bar. While others queue for coffee to drink on the coach, or rather the bus, I use the facilities, as Auntie Alison would say.

I go to the counter to buy something for Terry to eat. He is a big boy, probably fourteen; I think he fancies me, but he also treats me like a nine-year-old sister. I don't know which is worse.

I find a large cream bun which the lady puts into a paper bag. I think of brave Mister Bennet and the buns we shared.

While I sit on a bench outside the shop, people are sip their coffees at the tables inside and some sit on the bench with me.

It is like a rural scene in England in 1900. I see a pack of dogs with tails held high, prancing on their tiptoes. A cat is curled up lazily beside a bench. He opens one eye to check on the dogs, I see his body tense, ready to run. A horse is tied to a railing. Her rider, a brown wrinkled man in a check shirt and a cowboy hat goes into the shop.

It is Autumn here but the sun is hot. It is fiercer than the sun in the UK. I start to yawn. People are beginning to leave their tables to go back to the bus. It is time to take the cream bun to Terry.

I walk to the bus. Both the front door and the back door on the side of the bus are open. People have left valuable items in the bus. Is Terry honest? Is he a sneak thief, pretending to sleep so he can steal stuff?

No way. The man in the suit also stayed on the bus. He would have stopped Terry from stealing,

I pull myself up by the silver handrail. Mr Suit has gone. I look out the back window. I see him getting into a car. The rego plate begins LES, like my name. The car is an unusual type, perhaps a Volkswagen. I see the VW symbol and I know I am right. I like the light green colour.

"Terry, I bought you a cream bun."

Terry is slumped over, sound asleep, his back towards me. He has my girlie throw over him with just his head sticking out. I shake his shoulder. He tips towards the window then rolls and slides to the floor.

There is an open slash across his throat where his neck ought to be. My throw and his shirt are soaked in blood, glistening like wet plastic. He is dead.

I scream and scream and scream.

People hurry to the bus. A kind lady hugs my shoulders and pushes me away from where Terry lies dead. We leave the bus by the back door.

The lady and I sit on the kerbing with our feet in the gutter, She says, "Stay calm, stay calm little girl."

She is brown with large brown eyes like a horse, She rolls her eyes so the whites show. She smells nice, and her cuddles help calm me.

"Cops'll be here soon, dear. Keep to the truth even if it was you who killed him."

What?

"No. He was taking me to my Mum in Hastings. I didn't kill him."

"You get your Mum to get a lawyer. Smart, like."

I don't know if smart means quickly or clever, but I take out my phone and dial Mum, Mrs Lewis.

"Where are you, dear?" she asks.

"Mum, the boy sitting next to me has had his throat cut. We are waiting for the police."

"Do you know his name?"

"Tie Teatowel."

"Terry Te Tau, he is fourteen, year ten. A nice boy but quite naughty at times. You say he is dead?"

"Yes. Mrs?" I look at my helper.

"Mary Hepi."

"Mrs Meddy Heppee."

"Put her on the phone please, Lesley."

The two ladies talk. I am in shock and just switch out. An ambulance officer gives me a shake.

"Are you alright?"

"Yes. I am not hurt."

"What day is it today?"

I have no idea.

"You are in shock. Please come and sit in the ambulance. We'll take you to Napier Hospital for a checkup."

"Let me speak to my Mum."

Mrs Hepi hands the phone to me. "Mum, they are taking me to Napier Hospital for a check-up."

"Right. I'll see you there."

"Let's give you a small injection," says the ambulance man. They are called Hato Hone or Saint John.

Two minutes later I am fast asleep.

38.

"Are you awake?"

The voice comes from a woman like Fiona, a police officer in uniform but this one is light blue.

"Yes, I think so. Where am I?"

"In hospital. It is Thursday night at eleven o'clock."

"What happened?"

"You were given an injection to make you sleep."

"Why are you here?"

"I am Officer Julie Spence. I have to guard you. You are our only suspect at the moment. We have to clear you and guard you in case you were the target."

My heart sinks. I was the target. Mister Suit would be looking for a girl with red hair. Terry had the ends of his long hair tinted red. But he is a boy. Was a boy. Covered in my throw.

"Officer Julie, I think I was the target. Terry bought the tickets in my name. Lesley Lewis. Did someone in England send a message to Mister Suit to kill Lesley Lewis? Was Mister Suit watching Terry and heard him buy the tickets as Lesley Lewis?"

Officer Spence is silent for a moment. Then she accepts my ramblings as true.

"Who is Mister Suit?"

"A strange man in an office suit. He never smiled, never said anything. He stayed on the bus with Terry, who was asleep. I thought Terry might be faking so he could go on the rob. When I got on the bus, Mister Suit was down the road climbing into a pale green Volkswagen reg. beginning LES."

She takes out a notebook.

"Lesley, I want to take a statement from you. I need an adult to be with you. Give me a moment on the phone.

She rings Mum, Mrs Lewis.

We wait.

Two hours later Mum appears. She is very tall and has ginger hair, curly and full, not like my really red hair which is full and straight, She gives me a ginormous cuddle.

"My darling girl, I'm so pleased you are safe. Sorry it took me so long; its about a hundred and eighty kay. What happened?"

"After Terry was killed, I fell apart. A St John ambulance man gave me a jab. I woke up here. Mum, it is me they are after. It is a drug gang trying to keep John Smith quiet. The Russians would not have been so crude."

We separate. Officer Julie Spence takes over. I retell the story of Dad's imprisonment, his fears, the threat to kill me. I explain about the Russians and the Puka Elpa gang.

"For the camera, what's Puka Elpa?" asks Officer Spence.

"Dragon's Breath. They are big on dragons in Latvia."

My story is recorded on tape and Officer Spence takes notes. Mum says she is present and what is recorded is what has been said and she is prepared to sign a transcript as true.

"I think you are correct," says Officer Spence. "The Russians would have poisoned you. Totalitarian States are like that."

I get it. The name I couldn't remember. Toe tally tare ee an. Communist countries.

Officer Spence continues. "We will need to give you a new identity."

Oh no! Not another name.

"That will take about a month, with a New Zealand passport. The authorities in the UK will be notified and will give you a new

UK passport. The most difficult thing will be your height. You stand out."

Mum says, "Lesley is with us for a month, possibly permanently. She was a stolen child. I have just got her back. Do you have a name you would like, Lesley?"

"Yes, Lesley Benson."

Where did that come from? Fiona may not have me back if Brian and I can't live together. Should I choose Batchelor?

"That sounds fine. We'll go with that," says Officer Spence.

Mum is happy with that.

39.

I go home with Mum. The house is empty because Dad is in the office in town. Someone is looking after three year old George; the older two, Liam and Gerard, are at school.

When Robert Lewis comes home, he is just as he was on Messenger and WhatsApp. He is tall but not as tall as Susan.

He says to call them by their names, Susan and Robert. That makes life easier. I am tired and in shock so after I meet Liam, Gerard and George I go to bed.

After the weekend, I am enrolled at school as Lesley Benson. I like my class although it has more than thirty kids in it. The lessons are much the same. The teachers are much the same, except there is no-one like Miss Beech. There is a Civics elective on the same days. I join it and thoroughly enjoy it. There is a lot about gun safety, hunting and how to slit a pig's throat. Just what I needed, I don't think..

At school I don't see anything of Mrs Lewis. Nobody knows I am her daughter so they don't know I was sitting by Terry when he was killed. Terry's death has shocked everyone. School closes on the afternoon of his funeral. I go along with Susan but sit with my class. I cry.

"Why are you crying, new girl?" asks a narrow-faced white girl a year younger than me. "You don't know him."

"It's so sad," I reply. She shuts up.

The ladies of Terry's wider family, his whanau - it sounds like farno - sing and dance and wail sadly. The men do a haka. Then an old man, his grandad, says, "Where is Lesley?"

Everyone looks around. Nobody knows the new girl. I put my hand up.

The man pulls me forward.

"Thank you Lesley. You shared his last moments. You were with him just before he was killed. Your cool head let the police catch the killer. We are very grateful."

He put his forehead against mine and touched my nose with his. One by one all the whanau did the same. It was a massive experience I will remember all my life. Then there was another haka, the school one, I found out, and it was all over.

I found out later what Grandad meant. Mister Suit was arrested at Auckland Airport. If Officer Spence hadn't been quick, he would have been back in Europe.

The police traced a light green Volkswagen hire car with LES plates, went straight to the airport to check it for forensics, and to the check-in counter then the departure lounge. He was still wearing his hat and business suit. Now he is in gaol waiting for his trial for murder.

I have to record my story in a video interview because I might be back in the UK when there is a trial.

40.

It is Mum Susan's birthday. Although they asked me to call them Susan and Robert, the kids can't understand how I fit in.

Susan thought they would accept the idea that I was the first-born child and then was stolen. They didn't. They don't understand. They reject me.

The birthday is on Sunday. The Lewises go to church occasionally. On her birthday Susan takes the whole family to Holy Communion. I feel uncomfortable as I have not had my Confirmation. I get through it okay and we all go home.

We give our presents to Susan. I give her a lovely hairbrush. Her hair is red like mine so I know what kind is best. She is pleased. The kids give her cards they have made. Robert gives her a gold ring with a diamond set in a platinum clasp.

Then Liam fires a shot at me.

"Why does Lesley live with us? We don't like her. She is too bossy."

I tell them off when they are naughty. Susan said that was what big sisters do.

"When I am not with you, Lesley is in charge." she says.

"No she's NOT."

Liam is very angry.

"I hate her. I hate her."

I think he is angry because I stop his bullying of the younger ones.

So, Liam gets sent to his room. George cries constantly to support Liam. Susan is miserable.

"Can we leave you with the kids while Susan and I go to the pub to celebrate," Robert asks after the children are in bed.

"Sure," I tell him.

I face a constant barrage of whining and complaints organised by Liam, I put the two back to bed but they fight.

"Lesley, Gerard and George are fighting," screams Liam.

I get it. They want to taunt me until I hit them. There is no hitting or smacking in this home. I go to my room and lock the door.

Susan and Robert come home to chaos. The kids have tipped flour and sugar on the kitchen floor.

"What on Earth have you been doing?" Susan rages at me. "You are meant to control them; not let them do as they wish."

The kids make up a lot of lies about being in my room watching Netflix, and not coming when they were fighting. I try to tell her that the children decided to be as nasty as possible to me but she will not listen.

"I am very disappointed in you, Lesley," says Robert. "They are good kids and you let them go wild."

His comment hurts me the most of all.

Because of the problem with the children, and lack of support from Mister and Mrs Lewis, I decide to return to the UK.

Terry's funeral made me known by the whole school. They know I sat beside Terry and found him dead when I got on the bus after a coffee break. They are not surprised by my decision.

They are surprised when Mrs Lewis tells the morning assembly her daughter Lesley is returning to her home in the UK but will be back from time to time. She explains that I was stolen as a toddler and brought up by a kind family because I was too young to explain and the Lewis family had come to Hastings to teach.

She says that life is full of curve balls and education and courage are needed to overcome them. She says how proud she is of me, and asks for the assembly to sing 'Now is the Hour'.

Everyone sees me cry.

Embarrassing. Not.

41.

I fly home through Singapore. I have to stay overnight. It is really hot there. I swim in the hotel pool and have dinner on my own. It breaks the journey almost in half. That is the way I'll go in future. If I ever come back.

Auntie Alice meets me at Heathrow Airport and says Brian has gone. Shock horror. Was it because of me?

"No. Some firm investigated him and found he was already married. Fiona wasn't too upset, which surprised me."

When we get back to Wootton, Fiona seems as she always has been. It is as if I have never been away.

After catching up with my friends, I spend some time with Bill. He seems to have missed me, which makes me feel good.

I try to explain about the death on the bus. I am not sure he believes me.

"Bill, Mister Bennet is out of hospital now. Can you and I go to see him after school tomorrow? He says I must take some of his Spring bulbs and some seeds from his flowers."

I give Mister Bennet a call. He sounds frail and weak but is keen for Bill and me to visit.

We go the next day, after school. Mr Bennet moves slowly and sometimes stumbles. I feel sad.

We tidy up for him. When I do his bookcase, a box falls off the shelf. It holds his medals. I polish them for him. When I put them back, I see a gun covered by a black cloth on the shelf below.

I shudder. I hate guns. This looks like a gun he kept when he left the Navy. I cover the gun and put the medals back on the shelf above.

"I've polished your medals, Sam," I tell him.

"Thank you, lass. I wondered where I put them. Do me a favour and display them on my coffin, please."

"Oh, Sam, I might be married and living in New Zealand by then."

"Just say you'll do it, lass. Please. And don't let them put me in a home. I want to die here."

"Of course I will, Sam."

We sit at the table drinking tea. Bill is looking into space. I think he is not used to housework. Sam Bennet is sitting with his back to the bookcase. I am closest to the door.

I hear a clicking noise. I recognise the noise as someone picking a lock. The door swings open.

"Look out!" I scream.

Bill stands up as the door opens. A masked man stands in the doorway, He has a pistol in his hands. He waves it at us.

"Stay still."

Bill throws himself at the gunman, who fires at Bill. I scream and throw my tea at him. The hot water stops him for a moment.

There is a silence. Bill is moaning on the floor. Mister Bennet is standing at the end of the table.

"It's you I want," says the man, pointing the gun at me. "Sorry Lass; if you have the PIN to the bank account, give it to me now. Otherwise I have to kill you. Your Dad will not give Erich the pin number."

He is not Russian. He doesn't sound Latvian. He sounds ordinary English. He is a big man, too big for us to tackle. He is in a boiler suit, something he can take off and change his looks completely. But it is the gun in his hands that holds my attention. It is pointing at me. and his finger is squeezing the trigger.

I drop and roll under the table.

There is a very loud bang that almost shatters my eardrums. The large man in the boiler suit crashes to the floor right in front of my eyes.

His suit is no longer blue. There is a large red patch in the chest, I crawl out at the end of the table.

Mister Bennet's legs are in the way. He has fallen on to the tabletop. I wriggle past his legs.

"Mister Bennet! Mister Bennet!" I cry.

He doesn't answer. His face is turning white. His eyes are closed. I know what has happened. He shot the assassin with his Navy revolver. The shock of the attack has been too much for his heart. He is dead.

I go quickly to Bill. He has been shot but is not dead. His face is white with shock and pain.

"My arm," he says. "He shot my arm,"

I pull out my smartphone and dial 999. I comfort Bill and wait for the police.

Someone must have heard the shot and called them because I did not have long to wait for two female police officers to knock on the door. The ambulance arrives a short time later. I ask the younger officer to call Fiona and say I am alright and I am going with Bill to the hospital.

Bill is operated on. So Mister and Mrs Taylor can be at the operating room window, I sit in the waiting room, in a corner, with a cup of tea. Rose the Nose comes and sits beside me. She doesn't say anything, just joins me and sits silently. Nancy Drew arrives. She has had a growth spurt and is taller than me now. She throws her arms around me and I lean into her shoulder. It's great to have friends. We stay together until a doctor in a blood stained white coat tells us Bill is fine; the operation was successful and Bill's arm has been saved.

"He will sleep until early morning," Doctor Whitecoat says.

Mister and Mrs Taylor stand behind the doctor. When he leaves, they stay.

Mrs Taylor says, "Lesley, you poor dear. Are you alright?"

I think she is from Pakistan but I am too polite to ask her.

"Yes, Mrs Taylor. I am sorry Bill is hurt. He attacked the man and saved my life. He is a hero."

"Stupid boy, if you ask me," says Mister Taylor.

"Wouldn't you throw yourself at a killer to save my life, dear?" she asks.

"I s'pose," he says, but his eyes are laughing. They are both very proud of their son.

"Stupid man," she says.

"Run you all home?" he asks.

I fall asleep on the backseat of Mister Taylor's car. I wake up when Mrs Taylor gives me a shake. Our house is a semi-detached two-storey, like all the others in the housing development.

"Which one is it, Lesley?" she asks.

"The one on the left," I tell her.

I am alone on the backseat. Rose and Nancy are at their homes already. I try to get out of the car but my legs won't work. Mister Taylor lifts me up like a baby; I see where Bill gets his strength. He carries me into the house. It is not quite dark outside. Mister Taylor turns the lights on. Nobody is home.

"We can't leave you here alone," says Mrs Taylor. "I'll make a pot of tea."

There is a sound of a siren. A squad car is moving at speed, full red and blues flashing. It squeals to a halt. The passenger door opens and Fiona gets out and races towards the house.

"Lesley! Thank God you're safe!"

"Cup of tea, Ducks?" asks Mrs Taylor.

Things are back to normal.

42.

I don't go to school. Mister Bennet's niece phones me from Scotland. I tell her about the medals on the coffin. She will come to Wootton for the funeral and wants to meet me. She sounds nice but I have trouble understanding her accent.

A reporter wants my photo. He says Mister Bennet is a hero for saving a sailor's life. Now he wants to write about how he saved my life. Fiona says no

Fiona takes the whole day off. She is on her phone almost constantly. I sit in an armchair in the sun and think about my future.

I cannot stay with Fiona. Nor with Auntie Alison. The Russians or the Dragon's Breath gang will find me through them. I know they want to punish Dad because he won't give them the pin numbers, whatever they are.

It looks like I am homeless and friendless once again.

Name change, never to contact anyone from my past? A series of foster homes? No.

So, nobody knows who is trying to kill me but they have tried twice.

Hmmm.

What if Fiona and Auntie Alison and I have identity changes and go to live in New Zealand?

And lose my friends, my photo business, my school?

No way.

If I refuse an identity change?

They will kill me.

What should I do?